Your Name Is Joseph

Shaunté Newby

Copyright © 2024 Shaunté Newby
All rights reserved
First Edition

Fulton Books
Meadville, PA

Published by Fulton Books 2024

ISBN 979-8-89221-040-9 (paperback)
ISBN 979-8-89221-041-6 (digital)

Printed in the United States of America

This is to my dad and to all our family and friends. It definitely takes a village.

Special thank you to the staff at Sentara in Hampton and Riverside Rehabilitation in Newport News.

Introduction

Greetings and thank you for wanting a glimpse of this journey. My name is Shaunté Newby, also known as Shaunté Says, and I am the proud daughter of Janet Warthen and Joseph Newby. This book is about my father.

In 2015, he experienced an ischemic stroke and was in the hospital and a rehabilitation center for twenty-one days. I was there every day. A few days into it, I decided to keep a mini journal, jotting down observations, conversations, and some of my own personal feelings throughout this experience. I also have some tips that may be helpful to you if you are ever in this situation or one like it too. There were, of course, moments with tears, and there were some funny moments too. I wanted to have a way to show my dad what happened in case he was unable to recall any of this. I think of it like that night out with the one friend that didn't drink and can tell you what happened. So a majority of this is written as a journal addressed to him.

I am also a strong believer that our stories are not ours. So there is a least one person who needs to know that they are not alone in their feelings and experiences and possibly get a little humor out of it.

April 4, 2018
Three Years Later

Meghan, my sister, called me early today. I was a little concerned when I saw her picture on my phone since she and I had a bit of a disagreement a few days ago. So what came to my mind was, *Is something wrong with Dad?* It was via FaceTime, so I could see her face. She did the quick greeting, asking how I was doing. I answered that I was doing fine. Then she proceeded to say "Okay, now to the bad news." Silence. I froze for a millisecond. It is amazing how many thoughts can run through your head so quickly, but I remembered that I could see her face, so the news could not possibly be about Daddy.

She told me that Ms. Binky, or Debra, Dad's neighbor across the street had a stroke and was in the hospital. Her daughter was, of course, overwhelmed with what that all could mean. Meghan thought that maybe I could help or advise her since I experienced this with our dad. She explained how Ms. Debra was mentally stuck in the seventies. She thought her parents were still alive, but they died some years ago, and she thought her grown daughter was still a little girl.

After hearing all that, I thought about some of the things I did for Dad when he had his stroke. I shared a few ideas with Meghan to pass along to the daughter, like creating some note cards to post on the wall that would remind her what year it was and any other relevant facts. As I spouted out a few recommendations, my sister said, "You need to write that book we talked about a while ago. People need to see it."

So the book she was talking about is the one you are reading. What's interesting about this is that it was exactly three years ago on this day that Dad had his stroke. I had created an outline from some notes I took from that time to create a journal for my dad to see the experience from my point of view, capturing various moments, since I wasn't sure how much he would remember. I also thought that it could possibly serve as something good for other caregivers as well.

Hopefully, those who read this will be reminded to also take good care of themselves and do all that they can to prevent anything like this from occurring because it is life-changing, not just for the person who has the stroke but also for all who are around them, depending on the severity of it.

So much has happened in these three years, and I continue to believe that it is all by design and in God's plan. Just recently, I experienced some major life changes that have afforded me the time and ability to do this, so here we go.

But first, let me introduce you to my dad, Joseph. Some call him Newby, Joe, Boodoo, Buddy, or Boo. You may see some references to any of these names throughout this. My dad had his own barbershop for over twenty-five years, worked in the shipyard for about twenty-five plus years, and is also a Vietnam veteran. My dad and my mom divorced when I was three, and he never married anyone else after that. He's had girlfriends, but that's it. One sentence that I would use to describe him is from an old saying, "He never lets the grass grow under his feet." As you can imagine, he was always a mover and a shaker.

I decided to write this book years ago, but I just couldn't muster up whatever was needed to do it. Throughout the years, things would happen to remind me that I still needed to write this.

So here we go.

November 11, 2018

Dear Daddy,

It's Sunday, Veteran's Day, and it seems that I got another reminder to put this story out there.

You did something that was not like your usual pattern, and I got a little concerned. I called you several times, but you didn't answer. And actually, that wasn't the trigger.

Last night, after I left your house to return to Northern Virginia, you didn't call me. You usually call me before I even make it home to see if I made it safely, but I didn't get that call. So when I arrived home, I called you, but you didn't answer. Like I said, it was not usual, but I just told myself that you were possibly sleeping or out at the Zone, a local lounge.

Today, I waited a few hours until the afternoon. I told Mike how this is unusual that you didn't even call me back. I tried to call you a few times, and then the concern started building up with the thoughts about what could be going on with you. Mike suggested calling one of your girlfriends…the one I like the least…but I didn't like that idea too much because I didn't want to deal with her.

I called Meghan and told her my concerns. She said that she would go check on you for me. I could tell that it would not be right away, so I tried calling you again. I even called Nikki across the street, but her phone kept going to voicemail. *What is going on?* I just needed someone to tell me that they talked to you and that maybe they saw you too. Mike and I went back and forth as he was making suggestions for me to just call my least favorite of your girlfriends.

I don't know why I just worry about you dying and me finding out by not being able to reach you. It makes me panic.

You finally called me back. Sigh.

I don't know if you even understand how worried I get and why.

Okay, let me let you give you an understanding of what we've been through.

Saturday, April 4, 2015
Day 1

Dear Daddy,

    I think that there is no better place than this day to start to give you an idea of how today really went for me.

    I was cohosting a bridal shower for a close friend in Ellicott City, Maryland. I was going to be the maid of honor for her wedding that was scheduled in two weeks in the Dominican Republic. The bridal shower venue was at the bottom of a building, so my cell phone reception was poor, actually nonexistent. I didn't realize it until the shower was over and I went upstairs to head home. My phone started flashing with tons of notifications; many of them were from 757 numbers (Hampton, Virginia area code) not even saved in my phone. What in the world? What happened? I started listening to the voicemail messages:

"Your dad had a heart attack..."
"Your dad had a stroke..."

As I listened to each message, I slowly felt myself crumbling.

"Let me know how your dad is doing..."
"You must be out of the country..."

    What was odd was that after I listened to several of the messages, when I tried to dial out, I still couldn't make any calls. Guess I didn't make it to the better-signaled area yet. I freaked out and started crying. One of my closest friends grabbed the phone, and then we walked to a different area, and she dialed out for me. I ended up talking to a few of your friends. I asked to speak to you, and they handed you the phone. You sounded a little disjointed, but you knew who I was. I felt slightly relieved that I heard you, but I knew you weren't out of the woods yet.

I had to drive home to Northern Virginia to get my things so I could head down to Hampton, Virginia to you. Before I left the bridal shower venue, my friends asked me if I was okay to drive. I told them that I could do it, and I would be okay.

As I was driving, I called Mike, my boyfriend at the time, to let him know what was going on. He was very concerned because he could hear that I was still crying on the phone. He was actually coming from out of town that day and told me that he would be right over to take me down to Hampton. Of course, I tried to resist because you know I don't like to inconvenience anyone, but he insisted.

As I was waiting for him at my house, I started to hyperventilate, thinking about you, Dad. I was throwing clothes in a bag that didn't even match. I didn't even pack shirts. Sigh.

Mike picked me up, and as we were driving down to Hampton, your girlfriend, Anita, called. Your friends didn't want me to tell her what was going on with you. You already know that she isn't a crowd favorite. She called me because she was looking for you. You two were supposed to go to a dance later this evening. I chose to take the high road—even though she is not one of my favorites either—and told her what was going on with you. I told her that you were in the hospital, and you had a stroke. She was upset about your friends not telling her, but I got her to calm down and told her that I was on my way. She told me that she would be there too.

I will tell you this, Mike got me to Hampton in record time. It usually takes a little over two hours to get there. He got me there in under two hours! It was like NASCAR all the way down there.

When I walked into the hospital, I saw your brother and one of your good friends in the waiting area. They said that you were in the ER still, and they looked a little worried too.

I signed in at the counter, and they let me back there as it was limited to family and close friends in the ER, and only two were allowed at a time. Mike told me that he would wait for me because Anita was already back there with you.

As I was walking back there, I didn't know what to expect because my knowledge of what a stroke really is and does was very minimal. I just recall hearing about one's face possibly drooping. When I saw you, I was pleased to see that you "looked" okay. It was when you started talking that I could see how you were really doing. You said "faker, vader, vexer…" And you looked at us like we should know what you were saying. You looked scared once you realized that we didn't understand you. I tried to remain calm. The doctor came in and explained what was going on with you. I was told that you would have to stay in the hospital, in the ICU (intensive care unit).

After a couple of hours in the ER, they moved you to the ICU. As you can imagine, they had every vital you can think of being monitored. One that really stood out was the blood pressure. It was so high! I even saw it go over 200/100. When your blood pressure was elevated, alarms would sound. It happened every few minutes. The nurses told me that it was normal, and they were working to bring it down to lower levels, but it had to be done gradually or it could cause more damage.

As they were getting you situated, the nurse asked me to come in the hallway to talk about a few things. I was okay until she asked me to leave my information so they could call me if something happened to you. I literally fell out, thinking the worst, and Mike was there to catch me. He had to hold me up and calm me down. It just got real to me.

After I got my composure, I went back into your room. You told me in so many words to go get some rest because Mike and Michaela—Mike's daughter—were with me. Anita volunteered to stay the night with you.

I actually got a recap of that night from the nurse. They said that she was "a little much" while there. I figured that they were only complaining because she was there and probably asking for too much, but I learned that a patient not too far from your room was experiencing a Code Blue, and they were scrambling to address that. While they were doing that, she was yelling and screaming about your alarms and trying to get them to stop working with the other patient. But of course, there are multiple sides to every story. Deep down, I am happy that she stayed with you that night.

Sunday, April 5, 2015
Day 2

Dear Daddy,

    I went to your house to get your medication. You had so many pill bottles. I had no idea you were prescribed so much. I grabbed them all from the kitchen and from your bedroom. I told myself that when this was all said and done, I might have to box them up or at least sort through the old ones and throw out any old medication. My question to you is, Were you even taking your medicine?

    Later that morning, I got to meet Dr. Benis and Dr. Boulos. Dr. Boulos leaned over you and asked if you remembered his name. You told him that you didn't know it the first time you saw him. They laughed, and I laughed too. It was good to see that your sense of humor was still there. They explained some more of what happened and what their plan for you was. They explained to me that it was like a tornado went in your head and blew the "files" in your brain all over the place, and the road ahead consisted of trying to put things back the way they were as best as possible. At that point, I started taking copious notes in my little notebook.

    (Tip: Get a notebook to keep track of all that you are told and observe. So much is going on that it can be a blur, and when you need to refer to it, you will have it all there. Doctors' names, next steps, who you may need to contact, medications, etc. Years later, I still use this notebook.)

    I heard so many terms of things I needed to do and get: advanced directive, power of attorney, medical power of attorney. My head was spinning as I was capturing even more notes and actions.

    I learned that while I was out talking to the doctors and nurses, Mike said a prayer over you. You eventually told me that it was a powerful prayer and how right before he did it, he put some people out of the room. I know you always liked Mike, and he always liked you.

    Man, you had so many visitors. I knew that you knew a lot of people, but I didn't imagine all of them wanting to see you and being genuinely concerned. The ICU only allowed two people—besides me—at one time in the room, so everyone had to take turns going in there. People would come in to pray over you: pastors, deacons, you name it.

There was one deacon, I think her name was Ferguson, she prayed over you, and I guess she prayed over you again because when I entered the room, I heard her start to pray and you said, "Okay, again?" She said yes, then she aggressively put her hand on your head and started praying again. I chuckled to myself a little.

It got to the point that I decided to spend some time in the waiting area for some partial fresh air. As I was sitting there, thinking about everything that was going on, Anita came running out to the waiting area, screaming, "His blood pressure is over two hundred! Someone needs to do something!" It was like a scene in a movie. She had us thinking that you were coding out or something. When I went back there, the nurses talked to me, and they did say something about the number of visitors. I had to slow down the number of visitors. It was getting to be a bit much. I know I hurt some people's feelings, but it had to be done.

I had to text so many people to keep them updated on you. I would get so many requests to let them know how you were doing. I created a family group text that consisted of your brothers, your sisters, a few nieces, and nephews, and I created a text group for your friends. I just remember feeling like I was on my phone forever, texting people.

I ended up spending the night in the ICU with you. Mike and Michaela stayed too. I ended up in one chair, Mike in the other, and Michaela made a pallet on the floor.

It was a long and scary night for me. Those medical alarms had me on edge all night. You have sleep apnea, and when you stopped breathing at night, the alarms went off, and the screen turned red. The first time I heard and saw that, I almost lost it! I learned that night that the ICU was not where anyone got rest. It was wild. I am glad that Mike and Michaela were there with me. I have no idea what's ahead. I'm scared, Daddy.

Monday, April 6, 2015
Day 3

Good morning, Daddy!

Your name is Joseph. Today is April 6, and you are in a hospital.

I noticed that every time the doctors would come in, they would ask you a series of questions—including your name—to see how you were really doing. I thought that it would be a good idea for me to help you by starting your day with some of that info.

I woke up and took a shower in the hospital room. I have never done that before. It was kind of odd using that shower that was designed for someone who might need some help.

A little later that morning, a doctor returned to check on you. I asked about the high blood pressure since the alarms went off every couple of minutes. I was told that what they were doing was "permissive hypertension" and that your blood pressure would have to gradually decrease. I'm guessing hearing the words "permissive" helped me because that meant they knew it, and it was allowed.

Eventually, it was time for Mike and Michaela to leave and return to Northern Virginia. He didn't want to leave me until someone came to the hospital to relieve me. It was going to be a while, so I insisted that he headed back to beat that Sunday traffic.

I started thinking about your belongings when you were brought into the hospital and was told that security had it, and it would have to be released to me. I learned that you had a decent amount of cash on you. I never understood why you liked to walk around with so much money. That should have been in the bank. But I digress. So I requested the release, and part of the process was confirming with you that it was okay. They said that they needed to hear you say that I was your daughter. Oh boy. Let's see how that goes.

You were so confused.

The security person said, "Mr. Newby, who is this lady? Can we give her your items?"

You looked at the guy with a blank stare.

I screamed, "Daddy! Can they give me your stuff!"

It seemed like that snapped you out of it, and then you finally realized what was going on and said, "Oh, yes. That's my daughter. She can do whatever with it. I can't do anything anyway with it while I'm here."

So they released it to me.

It was your wallet, and it had all of your money, IDs, and credit cards.

I decided to take pictures of your identification cards since I would have to take care of your business and personal affairs.

(Tip: Take pictures of IDs and even credit cards. Save them on your phone. It comes in handy when you must handle business in many places.)

Anita came back, so I was able to run out and take care of some things. I wanted to make sure I got your money deposited in the bank. I also realized that I didn't have any more clean shirts left to wear. So I went over to Ross's to get a few. I always love deals!

After about a little over an hour, I returned to the hospital. I got to meet with a care coordinator. Her name was Paula. She let me know that she was there to do whatever I needed in getting you set up after you were discharged. She was so helpful and knowledgeable.

Based on the assessments, she said you really needed speech rehabilitation, and she recommended Riverside Rehabilitation, and the VA (veterans administration) would be backed up. I was so unaware of what having a stroke and the recovery entailed. It was really nice to have someone who answered all my questions.

Anita decided that she would spend the night with you again. Her conversations were so obnoxious. She was telling me that she was worried about you getting cleaned out, talking about your insurance and everything else. I just politely ended the conversation—as best as I could. I really tried.

I left and stayed at my mom's house. It was a bit difficult going to sleep. I asked my mom if I could get in the bed with her, and of course, she said yes. Yep, I was thirty-eight, and I crawled in the bed with my mom. You never get too old for that. It was comforting. She pulled the covers on me, and I tried to go to sleep.

As soon as I would close my eyes, I would be startled by the sound of the alarms in my dreams. I would jump or kick. When I opened my eyes, my mom was looking at me. She said, "Wow, you are not doing so good." Then I started crying and telling her about what was going on and how I was afraid for you, and I wasn't sure what would be the way forward. I also kept checking my phone all hours of the night, and Anita was sending these long play-by-play texts all night.

And of course, I got a recap from the nurses the following day. I was told that they could tell that she was getting on your nerves a little too.

Tuesday, April 7, 2015
Day 4

Dear Daddy,

Well, today started off pretty interesting. When I arrived, you were so happy to see me. You gave me a big hug. I couldn't understand what you said, but it was clear that you were happy to see me.

Later on, I was told that there was some bleeding from your bottom. They were concerned about the blood thinner they had been injecting in you, heparin. I was told that that gastrointestinal doctor would be coming in soon and scheduling a colonoscopy to see what was going on.

While I waited for that, I was advised to consider exercising FMLA (Family and Medical Leave Act). I decided to go out for a little while to make some phone calls. When I called my boss to let him know what was going on, he showed some concern, but at the time, it seemed like he was more concerned about when I was returning to work. He asked me, "Realistically, how long do you really need?" I told him that I didn't know, and I was actually irritated about that question because I wasn't sure how this was going to all play out with you.

More words were exchanged, and I recall being in tears because I didn't care about my job at the moment.

After I got my composure, I returned to your room. You started to talk to me as best as you could. Your words were a little jumbled, but overall, you said, "I don't think I want her around me until I get more energy."

I said, "You mean Anita?"

You nodded and said, "She bugs me. She worries me."

I just said okay and that I would let her know politely to back off a little.

Uncle Clifton came to see you today. You two were so funny. I guess as your big brother, it is his mission to pick on you. He told me that it was now his turn to mess with you because you picked on him while he was in the hospital, suffering from bone cancer. He said he was in so much pain, but you kept making him laugh.

I was glad that he was there with you. He made you laugh a little. He actually got a very comical reaction out of you when he leaned over and whispered in your ear, "I'm gonna come stay with you."

You opened your eyes so wide and said loudly, "*Heeeellllll nooooo!*" And then you started shaking your head like "No way!" It was so funny. You went from being so quiet and resting to almost screaming. We all laughed so hard.

He stayed for a little while, and then his son, CJ, picked him up to take him home. It was just you and I in the room, and you talked to me a little. You actually started to cry. You said, "Don't wear yourself out for me." And I told you that I was okay and that it was okay for you to cry. Then you started crying some more, saying repeatedly, "I don't know…" It was so hard to see you like that because you were still not really sure of what was going on with you.

Eventually, I got you to laugh about something. Then I pulled out my phone and said, "Let me take a selfie with you."

You looked at the phone with me and smiled.

When I showed you the picture, you said "Oooohhh, I need a beard."

I guess you meant you needed a shave. You definitely had more hair on your face than usual. I sent that picture to friends and family as part of my updates.

Eventually, Anita came back to see you. I asked to speak to her in the hallway and shared a little bit of your request to her, trying not to hurt her feelings. I just told her to lighten up a bit when she was around you. She stayed for a shorter visit this time. Maybe I didn't let her down gently enough.

It was starting to get late, and it was time for the nurse to come and get you cleaned up for the night. I went in the hall to give you some privacy. I overheard the nurse say, "Okay, Mr. Newby, I'm about to take your dentures out."

My eyes opened wide, and I went to the door and said, "Wait, he doesn't have dentures!"

She laughed and said, "I'm glad you said something because I was about to try to pull out his teeth. I asked him if he was wearing some, and he nodded his head."

I told her that you probably didn't understand what she said, which had been how it was since you had the stroke. I just shook my head and laughed. I wondered how long she would have tried to pull your teeth out.

I know I mentioned those alarms, but it is worth sharing again with you. You have been diagnosed with the condition sleep apnea. I didn't know what that was until you were in the hospital. When you stopped breathing while you were napping, the screens looked like you flatlined. You can imagine that scaring me a few times.

Wednesday, April 8, 2015
Day 5

Dear Daddy,

I didn't get that much sleep last night as you can imagine. I think you got a little bit of sleep. The nurses even joked and said you don't go to the ICU to get sleep. Those alarms went off all night, and sometimes, they were going for so long, and the nurses were so used to it that they knew when the alarms were critical to make moves. I got to the point that I would acknowledge your alarms myself since I was there. I saved them some time.

Today, you got a new nurse, Nurse Carmencia. She had a very thick accent.

"Mr. Newby, how are you today?"

You just looked at her, and then she said, "Maybe with my accent…"

I couldn't understand her either. I knew that this would be an interesting day.

She was pretty good, though. She said her goal was to get you moved out of the ICU to a regular room.

And you know what? It happened.

When it was time for you to move to another room, you said that you wanted to walk to your new room. You could only walk a short distance. You got a little tired, and not to mention, you had been in a bed for the past eight days.

As they were rolling you to your new room, you said, "I will be out of here in a few days!"

The nurses cheered. I think they all liked you. They said you were a good patient.

They moved you to room 316. It had a couch! I was able to spend the night there. What was nice and a little scary about this room was that they had the monitors at the nurse station. So there were no more alarms to keep us up at night, but there was the unknown. I had gotten so used to seeing your vitals and getting sense of how you were doing, and now I had to walk out to the nurses' station and look for your stats on their monitors.

Because I was so paranoid and worried about you possibly having another stroke, I found myself constantly going out there to see how you were looking on the monitors. The nurses were really nice there.

Before you were moved to that floor, I had expressed some concern, and I was told that they would have your room very close to the nurses' station until you improved a little more.

Thursday, April 9, 2015
Day 6

Dear Daddy,

    This will probably be on the list for one of the more eventful days in this journey. One we will talk for years and probably laugh about pieces of it.
    Today was the day for your colonoscopy. Whew...where do I begin?
    Before colonoscopies, you must take some sort of drink concoction (called MoviPrep), and I was told that it tasted terrible. I was told that you had to drink or ingest (keyword: ingest) it in scheduled intervals. You had been struggling comprehending anything since your stroke, and there was concern that you might not cooperate with the scheduled intervals. I asked what the options were to ensure that you get this done. They suggested the NG tube. I hesitated, but I knew that you had to get that concoction in your stomach before they could do the colonoscopy and confirm that you didn't have any internal bleeding. Then I gave the okay for them to do the tube. Why did I do that?
    So it was time to get the tube inserted. I was in the room with you, and a nurse came in with the tube. She proceeded to explain how she was going to insert it, and you would have to be calm and inhale and swallow as she was inserting it. Man, I thought the instructions alone were too much, but I guess this way would guarantee you get prepped for the colonoscopy. I held your hand as she was starting to insert it in your nose. You started panicking and screaming a little, waving your other hand. The room started spinning, and the next thing I knew, I was on the floor. I couldn't believe I fainted. I've never fainted before. The nurse was trying to hold the tube and trying to help me get up. I could see her trying to help me, and I got up and told her that I was okay. She said that I should probably leave the room. I did.

I don't know how I can watch surgeries on television, but when it comes to anything being done to a loved one, it feels different. I waited outside of the room and drank some water. I cried a little because I felt bad that they had to do that to you.

A few minutes later, she opened the door, and you had the tube in your nose. You were lying there with your eyes closed like you were recovering from being tortured. I think I even saw a little tear on the side of your eye.

The next nurse came in to give you the first dose of that MoviPrep concoction. Right through the tubes, straight to your stomach. They had do to it every hour on the hour.

The first few hours, everything was on schedule, but eventually, they got off track a bit, and I was concerned because that would delay when they could do the colonoscopy procedure. I went looking for a nurse to get the dosage, and it was like they all took a break at the same time. There was a nurse standing in for them, but she was from the maternity ward. She said she would call the nurse that was supposed to administer your last dosage. It was odd.

After about a little over an hour off schedule, a nurse showed up with the rest of your dosage. I was furious. Where in the hell were they! I was told that they were in a meeting. I expressed my concern, and the nurse apologized.

The goal of that preparation drink was to get your bowels cleared. Boy, did it! They had a portable toilet next to your bed. You would sit on it, shaking your head.

"No shame," you said, and you apologized about the smell.

What I did discover was that there was an air freshener that was amazing and cleared out the whole room's odor quickly. It was called Rainfresh Odor Eliminator. I looked it up on Amazon and ordered some. It was amazing. Thank God for that. You could clear a hospital floor with the way it was smelling in there.

Remember how I mentioned that the nurses fell off schedule with the preparation drink? Well, when it was time for them to take you down for your colonoscopy, they asked when the last dosage was taken. Because it was late, you had to wait longer for your procedure. We had to wait about two to three hours before they could take you back for your procedure. The doctor was not happy about that. He actually called down to the nurses and said a few choice words.

When they finally took you back for the procedure, I decided to check emails and make some calls. I spoke to my boss at the time, and I was given three options for my job: One, return as soon as possible, like a few days. We knew that wasn't happening. Two, resign and return later to try to find a new role. And I can't recall what the third option was. Needless to say, I was *not* resigning, and there was no way that I could return in a few days. Now I remember. The third option was for them to find a temporary backfill for me while I was gone. We went with that option. I let them know that I would be willing to talk to whomever if there were questions.

After about an hour, the nurses let me know that you were finished, and they would be wheeling you back to your hospital room shortly. They told me that everything was okay, and there was no internal bleeding. Thank you, Jesus!

I went back to see you. You asked if the tube could come out now. You asked a few times, and I said, "Not now, Daddy."

You were a little drowsy, but as they were wheeling you to your room, you asked for water. The nurse said that you couldn't have water yet, but you could have popsicles.

You smiled and said, "Can I get two?"

The nurse said, "Okay."

When we got back to the room, the nurse brought you four popsicles. You were so happy. You said something like, "I need to eat them all now before they hide them from me." I just shook my head and laughed. I then started recording you on my phone while you ate them. You looked like those popsicles tasted like a piece of heaven. You had your eyes closed and everything. I just laughed and smiled. It was good to see that you were okay.

After you enjoyed your popsicles, I sat down and looked at you. Then you said to me, "You were supposed to be tough." And then you started laughing. You were talking about me fainting as the nurse was inserting that tube. I just laughed with you.

I learned from the nurses that one of my longtime friends, Tyneka, dropped off Panera Bread and donuts for them "from the family." The nurses were so appreciative. I called Tyneka to let her know that the nurses said "thank you" and to also thank her myself. She mentioned how they brought the staff something like that when her brother was in the hospital. It was a gesture for thanking them.

(Tip: If possible, bring something like coffee or pastries for the staff. It is not only a good gesture, but they will also never forget it. They are caring for your loved ones. It is a quick and inexpensive way to show your gratitude.)

Later, I decided to video call a few folks. I called Meghan first. She was happy to see you but sad that she was so far away. She was in Kentucky at the time. I also called your brother Uncle Bernard. He was happy to see you, and he was watching you with your popsicle. I think it was the last one. Uncle Bernard just smiled and said, "I could just watch this for hours." I think he was relieved to see that you weren't as bad off as you were in the beginning. We made a few other calls to let people know how you were doing.

Big Tony, a very good friend of yours, offered to spend the night with you to let me get away from the hospital since it was such an eventful day. Anita came by, and you let her know in so many words that she didn't need to spend the night. She was a little offended, but she left. She mentioned to me that she would be leaving to go to Pittsburgh for her niece. Great timing!

So I left you there, and I knew you were in good hands with Tony. People don't mess around with Tony.

I went to my mom's house to get some sleep. I got a decent night's sleep. I learned later that they changed your room in the middle of the night. They were going to call me, but Tony advised them against it so it wouldn't scare me since it was the middle of the night. They moved you to the end of the hall, 307. That was a good sign for you. There was someone else who needed to be in that room closer to the nurses' station more than you.

Friday, April 10, 2015
Day 7

Dear Daddy,

 I got a decent amount of sleep last night. Tony called to give me an update about your move. Great news.

 I decided to go to your house to check on it. As I was walking through, I thought to myself, *Man, he has a lot of guns.* It was scary thinking about them being there when you got home. I didn't know what your state of mind really was. I didn't know if you would harm yourself or someone else. I had to figure out what to do with them. There was no more room in the case. I would figure something out.

 I came back to the hospital by midmorning. I could see you in the window waving at me and smiling, and the physical therapists were waving at me. Tony texted me saying that you were watching me as I parked the car. You said, "That's my baby girl!" I was told that you repeated that. It made me smile, seeing you at the window. The physical therapists helped you walk around the hospital floor. You were doing so much better.

 The doctor came in the room to see you and to let us know that you would be released today and could go home, and you had to have your blood thinner injected in your stomach for the next several days. What! Are they serious? How can they say it is time for you to go home! I was told earlier that you would be going to a stroke rehabilitation center. Why did that change? I didn't know what to do. I wasn't sure if I could take care of you, and I was concerned about you having another stroke. I read somewhere about the odds of having a recurring stroke are high, and not to mention, strokes are the second leading cause of death. So many thoughts were running in my head.

 I called Uncle Bernard because I wasn't sure what to do, and he, of course, told me to let him know if I needed him to come to Virginia from New Jersey. I told him I would keep him updated. I asked Tony what he thought, and I expressed my fears of trying to take care of you.

Tony said, "Just pray about it."

And I did.

I contacted the care coordinator who helped me a few days prior and told her what I was told. She checked into it, and apparently, there was a mix-up, and you would be going to rehab. Whatever the request was that she helped with got approved! Thank God!

We were told that you would be leaving at 3:00 p.m. Yay! It ended up being close to 5:00 p.m. While we waited, the speech therapists came in with iPads for your therapy. You still struggled with a lot of words, but they said you progressed a lot in a couple of days. They shared the apps with me so I could have them for you after you leave the hospital. Whew! It was expensive! But if it would help you, it was worth it.

They finally came in to get and transfer you. They had to take you by ambulance. Uncle Clifton just arrived, so he said he would ride with you there.

When you arrived at the rehabilitation center, they brought you in on a stretcher, sitting up and strapped in like Hannibal Lecter. It's funny thinking about it now.

As they were rolling you in, you looked around and said, "I know this place. I cut hair here and now…I'm here." Then you shook your head. I know you volunteered and cut hair for the patients periodically. You were always giving back.

You were admitted and processed by a tall nurse named John. As he went through your paperwork, he told us the rules, and they could identify your rule by your armband:

- Orange. Patient must be supervised unless patient is in bed and alarm is armed.
- Green. Patient can be alone if sitting in wheelchair but requires supervision with transfers and toileting.
- White. Patient can be alone except during transfers.

I learned that I could eventually get certified with transferring you, going from bed, wheelchair, walking, etc. You, of course, started with orange. You didn't understand why, but you followed the rules.

Your room had two beds, and the other was not occupied, so I was told that I could stay with you, and I did.

As I laid down to sleep, I was thanking God that you were able to be here in this facility. They got to inject that blood thinner in you, and we would not be alone if *anything* happened. I couldn't help but worry about you possibly having another stroke.

Saturday, April 11, 2015
Day 8

Dear Daddy,

    I noticed that every time nurses or doctors entered the room, they would ask you several questions: what was your name, when was your birthday, and sometimes, they even asked you if you knew who you were. You struggled answering those questions, but you caught on to the name question.

    I am amazed at this facility. They don't play around. Your initial therapy session was at 6:30 a.m.! Remember the rules? You have to get around in the wheelchair only. This session was actually with a group of some of the other patients at the facility. You all were impacted differently. At this session, they assessed your physical and speech capabilities. While the therapist was walking you around, some of the other patients said, "Wow, he's walking around pretty good." Most of the other patients couldn't walk. You had a pretty good initial session. Your speech was definitely the most impacted.

    After your session, we went back to your room. You got back in the bed. As you were lying there, you asked me, "What happened to me?" I told you that you had a stroke. I then showed you a booklet we got when you arrived, pointing to the pictures of the brain in the book. You then realized how serious it was, saying that you could have died. I just nodded my head, holding back a tear. Yep, even I didn't know how serious it was until I started reading up on it.

    Later on that morning, Mike called me via Skype while he was at my house putting together a bag for me since I didn't really bring down too much. After he gathered what I needed, he headed down to Newport News to see us. When he got here, I was so impressed that he even brought stuff that I needed but didn't think about, like my hair stuff. He packed extra stuff based on what he knew about me. Aww.

    Mike started talking to you to see how you were doing. I can see that you like him so much. Mike asked you for my hand in marriage.

I thought to myself, *What? What is going on?* Your response was priceless. You said in so many words, "I thought you would have done it by now. Shoot, you two may be married already for all I know." We laughed. We are not married. Then you both started talking about me like I wasn't in the room. You were talking about how strong and good I am. Sigh. I felt another tear coming. It feels like I have become a bit sappier since this ordeal.

Eventually, the conversation shifted, and Mike started working with you on your speech. He would write certain words and noticed that helped you a lot. I figured you were in good hands, so I took this as an opportunity to go out to get you some pj's, pants, and shirts.

While out, I grabbed markers and a journal for people to leave messages for you. I also picked up some index cards and some loose leaf paper. I had some ideas for those items that could hopefully help you.

Later that evening, Karen, KJ, came to see you too. She brings so much comedy wherever she goes. I know you both have a special place for each other in your hearts forever. I believe she tried to help you remember your birthdate. I think the nurse must have come in while she was there, and she saw how you struggled with answering those questions too. When I came back to the room, I noticed she had your birthday written out on the note card in different ways.

That night, I started writing the various answers for you to the commonly asked questions on those note cards I got. I wrote "Your Name is Joseph Newby," "You live in Hampton, Virginia," "You are currently in Riverside," and "The president is Barack Obama." Yes, they even asked you that several times. Sometimes, you remembered; other times, you didn't. Looking back, I don't think it was that you didn't remember. I think it was because you didn't understand what they were asking you.

I took those cards and started sticking them on the wall for you to see when you wake up. I put the one with your birthday up there too. I also put together a calendar on the wall so we could mark the days off, and you could see how much longer you have left. I actually did it to stop you from asking me over and over again if you were going home today. Yep, you asked a lot, sometimes a few times a day. When I put the calendar up, I pointed to your last day and said that was when you were going home. Having the calendar up also helped when they asked you if you knew what day it was. I had an arrow that I moved throughout the week, pointing to the days of the week. I think even without brain trauma, we can forget what day it is sometimes (smiles).

Putting up the cards helped, and it was done in time for your nightly medication. The nurse came in and, like clockwork, asked the series of questions. You looked at the wall and started answering them.

We made it another night. I like what I see here. The people are treating you so nicely. As I laid down, I still thought about you and wondered if you would ever get back to the you before the stroke. I said a prayer and cried a little because I wasn't sure how this would all turn out and what you would require after your time in rehabilitation. I'm still a little scared.

Sunday, April 12, 2015
Day 9

Dear Daddy,

When you woke up, I greeted you with "Good morning, Daddy, your name is Joseph. Today is Sunday, April 12." You looked at me and just nodded and said "okay."

Since it was Sunday, it was a light day. They offered a church service, but you didn't feel like going. We will try next weekend.

Derrick came to see you to cut your hair, but when he arrived, you were sleeping. So he waited for a while, and then he left.

Later that day, Ronald came to see you. You were up by then. You were so excited to see him, and he was relieved to see that you looked like you were okay. You called him Alonzo, his brother's name, a few times.

In conversation, you then told him that you "don't know what to say."

He looked at you and said, "Just say God is good."

You tried to say it. I then wrote it on a note card for you to read. When you read it, you said, "God is dead...God is dead..." You shook your head, and then you said, "God is good...God is good." Then you started tearing up and saying, "Yes, God is good." I couldn't help but tear up too. It definitely gave me some insight as to how jumbled up things were in your mind that the words were all mixed up for you.

Ronald stayed for a little while and then decided to leave to let you rest some.

You had to use the restroom. I hadn't been certified yet to supervise you getting out of the bed. We had to wait on the nurse to come in and take you the restroom. The LPN came in and took you to the bathroom. She left the door open the whole time. She said, "Let's talk about when you would like to take a shower." You didn't understand her, and she repeated herself a few times until you did. I tell you, it's wild seeing you like this.

Monday, April 13, 2015
Day 10

Dear Daddy,

The day started really early like it did on Saturday. This time, the occupational therapist showed up to get you out of bed. He had a really good personality.

He came in, saying, "Good morning, Mr. Newby. I'm Joe! I heard so many people talking about you."

You didn't understand what he was saying, but you were still pleasant. As you were looking to figure out what to put on, he said while he was pointing, "Put that Harley shirt on." You love Harley Davidson anything, so that was easy!

Then I think the greeting finally made sense to you because out of the blue, you said, "Your name is Joe, huh?"

And he nodded his head and smiled.

You got in the wheelchair, per the rules, and you were wheeled to your first real therapy sessions. I stuck around for these to see how they really went.

I was really impressed with the speech therapy. You have a long way to go, but with the way they conduct the sessions, I think they will help get you far.

After speech therapy, you had to go to physical therapy. That room was pretty extensive with all the simulated scenarios, like stairs and stuff. That session was interesting. They actually had you doing hip raises. I wonder if you had even done hip raises before this. I don't think you did. That was some serious work for you. I could see it in your eyes.

After those sessions, we went back to your room. That was where things started getting interesting again. I got a call about Uncle Melvin, your brother. Apparently, he had been involved in a motorcycle accident. I was careful not to say too much. Oh my God. Someone saw the motorcycle being carried away. I didn't know what to think. I called around to see what was going on and was told to call the police. Goodness. *What is going on?* I finally spoke to my Aunt Pat and learned that he was in the hospital waiting to be seen. It was pretty busy, and I guess there were many other people in worse condition. Eventually, I learned that he had some fractures in his back and some scrapes. My first instinct was to not tell you because I wasn't sure how you would handle it, and I was so concerned about stressing you out and possibly causing a stroke or something.

So I came back in your room and didn't tell you.

We decided to go outside for the first time since you got to the center. I had to push you in the wheelchair, per the rules. We went to the patio first on the first level. We sat there for a while, soaking up the sun. I could tell that you had a lot on your mind. Then we decided to go out to the grounds. We went to the gazebo and sat in there for a while. It was hard pushing you around on those ramps! But we got through it and made it back to your room in one piece.

I had a new mission for you: I needed to get you to drink more water. I guess I started shoving cups of water in your face a lot. You ended up telling me that I was trying to make you pee. Okay, maybe I was. But that was a good thing. I know you didn't drink as much as you should be drinking.

Later this evening, it was time for you to take a shower. The nurses came in to get you to take you down for your shower. When you came back, you were telling us in the best way you could about your experience, and it was funny. You shared how you felt a little funny with the young nurses seeing you naked, and you would stand there pretty much holding yourself so they couldn't see your private parts, like you were the first. Then you said how they scrubbed you down. I know that I can't do that story any justice, but it was funny when you told it.

Tuesday, April 14, 2015
Day 11

Dear Daddy,

Another eventful day at the rehabilitation center. The day started as normal with you getting up and getting dressed for the day. I decided to wash your clothes. Thankful that they had a laundry facility in the building. When I finished drying your clothes, I returned to your room and started to pull them out of the bag and fold them. Then it hit me: you can fold your own clothes! I handed them to you, and you just folded them like you were in the military. I laughed to myself as I thought about how I was going to fold them, but you are not helpless. You were so focused while folding them.

People were still coming in to visit you. So many people. But today, it seemed like everyone wanted to tell you about Uncle Melvin's accident. That was the first thing that your cousin Shine said as soon as he walked in the room. I always wondered why they called him Shine over the years. My mom told me that it was because of his complexion. Something about "he's so black he shines." Wow! I couldn't believe that. I thought the kids were mean when I was growing up. Okay, enough about that, focus, back to the hospital room.

This was one time that I was thankful that Shine speaks fast and indecipherably, and not to mention, you aren't immediately fully processing when people speak to you anyway. Any other time, you would have understood him. The running joke is that you are one of the only people who understands him.

Uncle Melvin didn't want you to know that he got into a motorcycle accident either. We didn't know what that would do to you. Keep in mind that you had been battling extremely high blood pressure since your stroke (and possibly before). We didn't want anything to push you over, and I feared you possibly having another stroke. So I was okay with not telling you too.

It was time for physical therapy again. Today, they had you doing squats. I don't think you have done squats in a *long* time. I even told the therapist that you didn't do stuff like that, so you would definitely feel it! When the therapist started walking with you, she grabbed your arm, and you looked at her and smiled. You said, "Are you flirting with me?" You are so funny even with all that is going on.

I decided to leave and take care of some of your business stuff while you were in therapy. I knew that you would have to go to speech therapy after the physical one. I went to have a meeting with Scott and Mike at the barbershop. It wasn't pretty. I expressed my disappointment in how they let things go while you were not there, and it was unacceptable.

After I left your barbershop, I decided to return to the center to check on you. When I walked in, you were sitting in your wheelchair, and you were sleeping. I tapped you on your shoulder, and with your eyes closed, you said, "XYZ, ABC…ABC, XYZ." I chuckled a little. I can tell that speech therapy took a lot out of you!

We decided to go the multipurpose room to play some games. They had a Wii in there. Oh boy…I remember how you kicked my butt in Wii bowling a while back. Perfect score! I wonder if you remember how to play. It looked like you did remember. You grabbed the remote and closed one of our eyes to aim. The stroke impacted the vision in one of your eyes. I am guessing the one you kept open was the one that was the strongest.

After we played for a little while, we decided it was time to head back to your room. You got a phone call from your lady friend, Anita. She was talking a mile a minute like usual. You looked at me and shook your head. Then you handed me the phone while she was talking and said, "I don't know what she is saying." It was funny because it was her, and it was not funny because you couldn't understand her like you did before. I just told her that you were tired, and you were having a hard time understanding her. She sounded disappointed. Then we got off the phone.

Dad, I tell you that going through this experience has shown me a lot. It showed me who truly cared for you and even who truly cared for me. I may not have gotten a chance to mention it in the earlier journal entries.

Today, my best friend, Artisia—you call her the professor—brought me something to eat. She also brought me stuff I asked her to print for your taxes. We only have a few days until it is time to file. I guess I could have gotten an extension, but I didn't want it to be late.

While she was there, I got a few minutes to talk to her, and I was just so thankful for the love and support from her and our other friends. I even mentioned how Mike stepped up and just showed me that he truly has my back. She said to me that "when it's the darkest, the brightest stars will shine." She was so right. You have so many stars around you. I have so many stars around me. I feel truly blessed.

After she left, it was almost time for you to turn in for the night. I had made a request to get some changes to your CPAP machine. I told the respiratory specialist how the piece that covered your nose and mouth was drying you out. I almost had to argue with the lady, but I wanted to be mindful that these folks were taking care of you. She finally listened and got a piece that just went in your nose. It was kinda funny. It made you look like a pig. But you said it felt a lot better!

Wednesday, April 15, 2015
Day 12

Dear Daddy,

You did your usual therapy this morning. It was a little too cool outside, so we didn't go outside today.

At the end of the hall on your floor, there was an area that had puzzles and other activities and beautiful view of the water outside of the facility. With you in the wheelchair, we went down there, and there was a gentleman in a wheelchair sitting alone, named Kyle. He looked very sad.

You started talking to him, and I just watched. You told him how you had a stroke, and you noticed that he couldn't move his leg, so you asked, "What happened to you?"

He told you that he had a stroke, and he couldn't walk.

You looked around sneakily while in your wheelchair and said, "I can walk," like you were letting him knew that you could help him. You then proceeded to rub his leg and lift it, moving it around.

Kyle smiled and said, "Man, you should be a therapist."

You continued talking to him, and I heard you tell him, "Don't sit alone. Talk to people. Talk to me."

You made his day. Even with all that you have going on, you found a way to be helpful and kind to someone. I was so proud of you.

I got certified to let you walk around with me. This is a big step! I just had to demonstrate that you would listen to me, and I could keep you safe. I know you were happy with that as that reduced some of the restrictions like having to stay in your bed or only be in the wheelchair.

One of your old barbers, Jason, reached out to me. He said he wants to come back to the barbershop to work for you. He still needs to get his license, though. I mentioned this to you, and you said that he can return only if he's clean. I saw him recently, and I don't really know if I can answer that. So I'm thinking that we are going to wait about Jason, and I heard you telling people on the phone that he's coming back. I could only shake my head. Can I blame that on the stroke? You probably would have done the same thing prior.

Remember when I mentioned some of your good friends? Well, Martha, Big Man's wife, offered to clean your house to help get it ready for you to come home. I also asked Tony, Big Man, to help me secure your firearms. You have so many everywhere! I wasn't sure what state of mind you would be in when you got home. I guess my mind ran in some of every direction. I wasn't sure if you would be depressed and possibly think about…harming yourself or harming anyone. Even as I write this, I tear up. I know that this stroke is life-changing for you, and life as you knew it before April 4 is different. So I wanted all the firearms out of your house. Call me crazy, but I was just worried about them being in there.

By the evening, it looked like you were making significant progress with your blood pressure and everything else. The medical staff said they could see some improvements, and everyone who came to visit you frequently said they could see it too. Thank you, God!

That evening, Anita called you again. You held a quick conversation with her and handed me the phone. You still didn't want her to come around until you got through this.

Your dirty clothes were accumulating again, and I mentioned how some of your friends offered to wash the clothes for us. You told me that you didn't want your friends doing the laundry. So we both took a walk down the hall and washed your clothes.

It's Tax Day…I think I got everything done on time, your taxes and mine!

Thursday, April 16, 2015
Day 13

Dear Daddy,

Today, I would have been on my way to the Dominican Republic to be in my friend Nakia's wedding on Friday. She was the one whom I was cohosting the shower for on the day you had your stroke and no one could reach me. Of course, I wanted to go to Dominican Republic, but you are more important, and I couldn't just leave you like that. I didn't even care that I lost all the travel payments, hotel reservations, and plane tickets. It didn't even matter. Family first!

You went to your regularly scheduled therapy session. When you returned, you told me how you didn't understand something. You then started to cite out the days of the week, using your fingers to count them. "Monday, Tuesday, Wednesday, Thursday…I don't get it." I wasn't sure what you didn't understand, but I made sure I pointed to the wall with the calendar I made that had the days of the week on there.

Nurse Jennifer commented about all the stuff I had on the wall for you. She said that she has never seen the families of other patients do things like this. She said that it is really helpful. I told her that I was determined to do what I could to get you back close to normal as possible!

I finally got to wash my hair after two weeks. It was a lot of shedding. I am guessing that some of it was due to stress and the rest it being dirty.

I picked up some of your clippers and a picture for you to help you with some memories. You were insistent about being able to cut your own hair. You told me that you wanted to cut your hair before they came with your medication. I guess you knew that it could possibly affect your energy. So I handed you the clippers, and you took them into the bathroom. You unraveled the cord, and the plug fell into the toilet. You then grabbed it and was about to just plug it in. I ran in to stop you and grabbed it to dry it off. I was so shaken but tried to stay calm. All I could think about was what would have happened if I was not there. Sigh. But you know what? I was there, so all is well. But it was so scary. You didn't fully understand and looked at me a little funny. That actually bothered me too. You didn't know what kind of danger you were possibly in with the plug falling into the toilet. Thankfully, I was there.

As usual, you got a lot of visitors. Moon Mullens, but you kept calling him Boon Boon (may he rest in peace now), the ninety-two-year-old Navy vet who doesn't look ninety-two! He was actually at the barbershop when you had the stroke. He comes by a lot to check on you. Some other folks came too. They all would ask the same thing when they saw you: "Do you remember me?" Folks just want to be remembered. Some people were friends of friends who came to see you.

One guy came by who was a friend of a friend. He even asked if you knew him. You said to him, "I'm sorry, I don't know you." You looked puzzled, and you looked like you actually felt bad for the guy.

After he left, you looked at me and said, "I know a lot of people, but I don't know that guy." I could only laugh. I think he told me that you two have a mutual friend. And maybe you ended up at the same event one day. It's pretty amazing that someone met you one time and wanted to come see you at the rehab center. I keep learning more and more about you as more people come to see you.

Derrick, a good friend of yours, came to see you. It was pretty funny actually. He asked you if you could hear him. And I don't know if you were playing along, but you acted like you couldn't understand him. He then told me to write it down for you and pointed to himself. Then you started laughing.

I keep telling folks that you can hear; you just can't understand them sometimes.

We finally got your discharge date! It's April 24, Friday. That's good. You asked about going home every day! I think you will continue to. So I marked it on our homemade calendar with note cards and made a little sticker move through the dates to help with the countdown. You actually looked on there and started counting the days. Then when you realized it meant a whole week left, you said, "Goooooottt daamn," snapping your fingers and shaking your head.

I just laughed. At least, you won't be asking me every day; you will look at your calendar.

That calendar was also helpful when the nurses would come in to check on you. They would go through their usual series of questions: what's your name, when's your date of birth, what is today, who is the president, stuff like that. When you weren't sure, you would look at me, and I would then look over to the wall with all the note cards with messages and our infamous calendar. You responded, "Oh, she wants to know my birthday? October 6." It worked! What's funny to me is that for people who have not experienced a stroke, they may not even know what date it is…sigh.

I kept telling you that you need to drink more water. You would resist and tell me that I was trying to get you to pee on yourself. Finally, you just caved in and said, "Okay, give me the water." It was my mission to help get you on to some good habits.

Anita called again. She asked if you wanted her to spend the night with you at the rehab center. You said no, and you still kept saying that you don't want her around until you get through this.

Karen came by to check on you. While she was there, I decided to step out to get a quick break and some fresh air. I went out to grab something to eat. When I returned, I learned that you two talked about selling corn liquor (moonshine) on eBay. What? Okay…she always brings out the fun when she's around.

After she left, the nurse came in to do your medicine. We mentioned to her that you had a little bit of blood in your urine. We were told that it might happen because you were on heparin (blood thinner). You pulled your pants down to let her see the spots on your underwear. She said she would let the doctors know but she thinks you're okay.

After the nurse left, you folded all your laundry. I keep reminding myself to let you do as much for yourself as possible.

Tony and Martha came by and brought me a blanket since you took mine. That was so nice and thoughtful of them. They have really been there for us!

As it was time to call it a night, I got in a little argument via text with Mike. Apparently, he was bothered that I didn't call him back. Okay, I will deal with that tomorrow.

Friday, April 17, 2015
Day 14

Dear Daddy,

Today, I was asked to get you up and ready. Of course, it's not as bad as it sounds. You listen to me. So I started with my usual "Good morning, Daddy!" routine.

You got up, washed up, and put your clothes on for the day. I didn't mention it, but I think I brought all Harley Davidson shirts for you. It's a conversation piece no matter where we are in the facility. "Oh, you ride Harley's," and then you would usually smile and say "yes." I would then add "He's one of the best riders I know, and I am not just saying that because he's my dad." It's true. Ask anyone who knows you; they are always in awe when you ride.

I think about how you used to put me in front of you on the motorcycle so I would be in between you, your arms, and the handlebar. Then you would take me for a ride and do wheelies. I was only two. I think you did that until I was about four. My mom told me that she would always be scared to death, and I would always ask you to do it again. Sigh…I actually remember it so vividly. Big gold helmet on my head and I would be holding on to the middle part of the handlebars. You would ask me, "Are you okay?" and I would scream, "Yes, do it again!" I remember seeing the sky when you would do that.

Okay, back to the facility.

So when people noticed the shirt and asked you questions, I felt that it made you feel good to talk about riding, and you would also say, "My daughter rides one too. A big one." Then folks would ask more questions. I always like the opportunities that would make you almost forget about where you are and what has happened to you.

We went back to your room after breakfast and just sat around watching TV. I could hear the man next door yelling, "*I don't need your help!*" He was yelling at his lady. I don't know if she was his wife or girlfriend, and that didn't matter. But I know that he did need her help. I guess he was just going through his range of emotion about his situation. I imagine that even though she knew he was not his usual self, it had to hurt to hear him yelling at her like that. I saw her walk out of the room past your door. Probably needed some fresh air and considered leaving his butt there alone.

You went to the bathroom to poop, and when you finished, you came out and stopped for a second. You said, "It doesn't make sense. I just came out, and now I have to go again, and that don't make any sense." Poor thing. I guess it may be the medicine. Hopefully, it will work its way out…literally, LOL.

I decided to call the VA (veterans administration) since we got your official discharge date. They gave me the runaround on the phone, and you could hear it. When I finished the call, you said, "Everybody is busy…all the doctors are busy." I could only nod. I tried not to show too much of my frustration to you because I didn't want you feeling bad about all that is going on. I know you did mention, though, in so many words that you weren't looking forward to seeing your primary doctor because she told you this (stroke) would happen. I have to admit that I had no idea about your health and the amount of medication you were taking before you had the stroke. I had no idea.

As I was sitting there, I thought about your health and how your life has completely changed. To get through this, you will have to make some changes too. I took the index cards with the markers. As I was writing, I was saying things to you like "Dad, your life is different now. You will need to make some life changes." So I wrote in all caps "LIFE CHANGES" on one card. I then said, "No stress." I wrote that on the card. Whew, that's a loaded one!

I truly feel that your current relationship with Anita is a big chunk of that. I am not with you two all of the time, but when I am, it doesn't feel like a positive dynamic. I also feel like some choices you made with the barbershop added to your stress too.

"Don't worry." That one goes well with the first statement. "Rest. Relax. Eat Healthy. Exercise. Drink Water. Take Medicine." I wrote each of those on a card, and then I stuck them on the wall like a list. It was like you were in class as my student. I read them to you and asked you to read and repeat them as best as you could. You said "Yes, ma'am!" and did what I asked, and then you nodded in agreement.

(Tip: Words have power. Use note cards to write words of encouragement for your loved one.)

Nurse Jennifer came in to check on you. She said you were one of her favorites, and she really likes working with you. I think all the nurses like working with you. They would have to rotate on the floor, caring for different patients, and the ones who weren't responsible for you would still make their way to your room to say hi. You're like a celebrity in here.

Later on, I decided that we should go out and get some fresh air. I am able to take you outside without having to do too much formal stuff now. We still had to use the wheelchair to get around, though. I had to push you. Those ramps gave my legs a workout!

As I was pushing you on one of the sidewalks, I almost made you topple out of the chair. Thankfully, you didn't! We both laughed. Then you asked me if you could just push me around in the chair instead. No way, man! I am *not* trying to lose my recently gained privileges in that rehab center.

I tried to help you unlock your phone. You don't remember the pattern to unlock it. After so many attempts to unlock it, the phone ended up resetting. I don't think you had too many things on there that would be lost. Inadvertently, you have your stuff backed up on Google. (Thank you, folks, at Verizon!)

We returned to your room. You had a lot of visitors today.

Yvonne B. came by to see you. She brought you a plant. I just smiled and jokingly said, "Great, one more thing to take care of." I don't mind telling anyone that I am *not* a plant person. I am 007 with plants. I have even killed bamboo…how do you do that? But it was a nice gesture, and we are grateful!

She was telling us how she was getting a new motorcycle. You couldn't understand what she was saying, so I tried to help out and repeat it. You still didn't understand. You started getting frustrated. Then your eyes started tearing up, and you said, "I don't like this."

Yvonne and I both told you that it was okay and that it was not a biggie. I told you that we would just talk about it later. I don't know.

I am thinking you thought we were telling you that something was wrong, but you didn't understand or maybe it was just because you didn't understand. It's like it turns on and off for you. Sometimes, there are moments when you seem to be flowing and keeping up, and then there are times when you look at us like we are speaking another language. It must be scary. I think you were getting a little tired too.

So, like I said, you had a lot of visitors today. It was so many that the people at the front desk knew to just write your name on people's visitor stickers. It always seemed like the ones who visited for the first time would ask you if you remember them, and then they would reminisce about some old stories. They kept asking you about the past. It was a bit annoying. I understand that people are concerned for you, so I try to politely tell them that your memory is fine. In my head, I am screaming, "*Damn it! His memory is fine! I need him to process what he is hearing!*" Deep breaths…they don't know any better.

I will tell you that I don't know how I feel about you telling everybody about how I passed out that day when you were getting the tube in your nose. You tell it the same way every time. "You were supposed to be tough, Shaunté, and you passed out!" Then you would laugh, and your friends would laugh too. It is kinda funny, though.

Shine called. He told me to tell you that one of your friends called Fat Ricks died. I still don't know how to share news like that with you. I know you knew that he was actually in the hospital the same time as you were right after you had your stroke. Right now, I am choosing not to let you know about that. I feel that you have a lot on your mind, and I have seen you emotional about your own situation. I didn't want to add that to you. Is that the right thing to do? I don't know. Plus, it's hard to explain things to you these days. You seem to get a little frustrated because you don't understand. And I am worried about your blood pressure. So I will hold off on that.

Mike called me. When I told you that he was on the phone, you smiled and said, "Your husband…my boy…my best friend!" Mind you, we are just dating. I just shook my head and smiled. I love that you two get along so well. That was a short conversation, but you ended up smiling and laughing a bit with him. I wonder how much you understood from that conversation. Whatever it was, you left it laughing. At this point, what was said doesn't matter. I am just happy that you are in good spirits for the moment.

Troy, our cousin Jan's husband—so that makes him our cousin too—came by to see you. You were so focused on the days of the week. He started telling you about a friend of yours named D who also had a stroke not too long ago. It wasn't funny at the time, but your responses didn't match the conversation when it was happening. You started saying, "Monday, Tuesday, Wednesday, Thursday, Friday, Saturday, Sunday…Yay, I got it right! Okay, again, Tuesday, Thursday, Saturday…Shit, I just had it right!" You then told us how you dream about words and say all the days of the week. Eventually, you got back to the conversation about D. You looked shocked because he is so much younger than you. I guess strokes do *not* discriminate.

The nurses walked in, and it was time for you to take your shower for the night. You asked if you should poop first. You're silly. Troy took that as his cue to head out. After he left, the ladies took you for your shower. If I didn't know any better, I think you enjoy that part of your stay. You seem to make the nurses laugh every time. I imagine that eases some of the possible awkwardness. Maybe that's just me.

When you returned from your shower, dressed in your pj's, we talked for a little while. You talked to me about your physical and occupational therapy. You said that you would get through all your activities so quickly, and you would end up sitting there with nothing left to do. You told me that you just do what you are told. And then you said, "I may joke, but I am blessed." Yes, Daddy, you are.

It's amazing how when I start feeling bad for you and what's going on, you find a way to bring humor in this.

It was getting late, and you are now asking for your CPAP machine. I think you are willing to do anything that you even think will help you get better!

As you dozed off, I laid down in the extra bed in the room. Despite your perspective you shared on being blessed, I couldn't help but break down. Life as I imagined for you is different. I started thinking of how will things be for you going forward. You were a barber with your own business, calling your own shots, and now you can't even understand a fraction of what people are saying to you. Millions of thoughts ran through my head. I am worried that I may not be able to take care of you to the level that you need. I talked to Mike again that night on the phone. I admit, I did a little nit-picking with him, but I don't think I was wrong. Well, maybe I was just on edge.

Saturday, April 18, 2015
Day 15

Dear Daddy,

Today, I got you up and ready since I am here. Nurses have less to do now. When one of the nurses stopped by, I laughed and said that they needed to pay me now since they didn't have to do as much with you. However, the showers, they can keep that task. Ha ha ha.

We went to the dining hall to get breakfast. There was a gentleman there named Kyle. He was crying. It was his birthday, and he felt "weepy." We wished him a happy birthday.

In conversation, we learned that he used to be an airplane mechanic. He didn't think he would be able to return to it after his stroke. I started trying to think about some other things he could possibly do.

I said, "It's possible for you to stay in the same field but do something different like training people or even be a QC (quality control) person."

He quickly responded, "I don't like those guys..."

I just smiled and said, "Well, you can be what you think they should be."

He smiled and said, "You know what? You're right."

It felt good to see his energy change in that conversation. It was like he had some more hope beyond his current situation. I truly enjoy helping people see beyond what they normally can see. So even though I was not at work, I was still able to do some things I love doing.

After breakfast, we went back to your room. You asked me what I was doing for myself today. I told you that I was hanging with you today. You told me that I could go out for a little while to get a break. I guess you felt a little bad that I was there with you, but I didn't want to go anywhere else.

I had been texting with Meghan. She said that she might be moving back to this area permanently. I am not sure what's going on, but she said she would share more later. I hope that everything is okay.

So you and I had a lazy Saturday together. I was lying down in the second bed, and when I looked at you, you asked me what I was thinking at that moment. I responded with a simple, "I just want to make sure you are okay." You then said that when you look at me, you wonder what I would be doing if you weren't sick. I just did a small smile and said, "Probably the same thing I am doing now, being lazy." And then I laughed. You smiled a little, but I know that was heavy on your mind. I didn't want you to worry about me right then.

Anita is back. She asked if you knew her name. You just looked at her for a second, and I guess you didn't respond quick enough. She then said, "You used to call me NeNe."

Then you just nodded an agreed with a "yep."

Then she started looking at the pictures on the dresser, looking for hers.

You said, "Yes, your picture is up there too. I see you looking. My daughter brought it."

She has an idea of how I feel about her so that probably shocked her a little.

She told you that she was in town for a little while. I was trying to figure out if I could leave you with her for a little while, but I worried that you would try to show off for her, letting her know that you weren't really feeling that bad.

A lady came by to take your food order. She asked what you wanted after she listed out all the meals options that were available. You asked her to say them again, and she did. I am sure that she is used to having to do that. It's challenging sometimes to just sit back and let you be with this condition and not take over, but I try to let you have as much independence as possible, so this time, I didn't say anything. It was funny when she mentioned ham as one of the options, and you couldn't understand it at first until she repeated it. Then you said, "*No ham, no way. No, ma'am!*" You picked the turkey.

I guess you were thinking about how the ham might have more sodium. I realized, though, that their options were catered to your needs, which was based on hypertension. So, technically, you could have had the ham. Sorry. I am sure that it probably doesn't taste as good as yours, so you didn't really miss anything. Also, I think avoiding pork or at least eating less of it may not be a bad shot for you.

A little later, an older gentleman that goes by Chief came to see you. I learned that he is ninety-two years old. He's an interesting man, and you definitely can't tell that he's ninety-two. It seems like he comes by every other day or so to see you. Apparently, he was there the day you had your stroke.

Some of your cousins came by too. You called one of them Boss Dick, and you kept saying it. I guess it didn't sound right to you, and it wasn't his name, *but* it was close. His real name was Bill Dicc. Whew…at first, I was wondering why you kept saying Boss Dick. It was close.

You still talk trash to non-Harley Davidson riders. I think folks weren't expecting you to have the same sense of humor after the stroke. I'm sure they were a little relieved, even if you were picking on them. It's all love. I actually like seeing you like this too. It's a sense of relief for me.

Someone mentioned the restaurant Surf Riders. At first, you didn't understand what they were saying. I wrote it down on a piece of paper. You then yelled, "*Surf Riders!*" You love that place. You almost jumped out of the bed.

Eventually, everyone left. Anita hung around for a little, and then she left too.

You looked a little puzzled after everyone left. You asked me why had people been talking about the past so much. I was wondering the same thing, but then as I think about it a little more, I am guessing they did that because they were scared and thought about how we almost lost you. The more I think about it, I got an opportunity to learn more and more about you from the perspectives of others. I learned even more about your sense of humor, your generosity, and even your temperament.

After a little bit, I decided that it was probably a good time to go out and get some fresh air. You still have to go places in the wheelchair for safety reasons. As I was struggling to push you up the inclines, you asked me if you could just push the chair to help me. I, of course, refused. I didn't want to lose any of the privileges I gained.

As we were outside, the sun was beaming. I noticed that I forgot to grab a hat for you. I was so nervous about you possibly having another stroke. All I could think about was if it was too hot for your head and it wasn't protected. So I turned the wheelchair around to go back and get it. We had to face those inclines again after we got your hat. I got a serious leg workout! We stayed outside for a bit. I took a few "usies" (group selfie) while out there. The facility is near the water, so being outside is very peaceful.

We went back in after about an hour or so.

Nurse Leslie came in to check on you. He was a pretty cool man. You complimented his beard. I let him know that you are a barber, so a compliment like that is a little more than the usual. He rides a Harley too, Fat Boy. So that lead to even more conversation. Very nice guy.

Martha and Tony came by. They brought the money from the barbershop. They were so pleased to see your improvement. I can see that they love you, and you love them too. Martha wants your plant from Yvonne. They stayed for a little while, laughing and talking. Somehow, Chitlins came up in the conversation. You said, "I won't eat them, but I know they are good," then you looked around and said, "Maybe I can eat a little bit." There goes that giving up pork. I think it lasted a few hours! Of course, we all laughed.

After Tony and Martha left, my mom and Aunt Kitty came through. Mom bought me some stuff like clothes. You were telling them about how I have been there for you this whole time. You even said that you weren't sure if I still had a job. I just shook my head. Aunt Kitty prayed for you, rubbing oil on your head. I think this was actually the third round of prayers for you. You were keeping count too. The first was a deacon from your church and then your biker cousins and, finally, Aunt Kitty. Honestly, you can never have too many prayers, especially in a time like this.

Mom told you that she still loved you. That caught me off guard. I never thought I would hear her tell you that. I always knew that she did, but it was definitely a touchy subject. Life-threatening incidents bring out the truth in people, it seems.

After they left, you gave your oldest brother, Clifton, a call. When you talked to him, you called him by his nickname, Hambone. He said that he could hear the difference, and you are sounding more and more like your old self.

It was a long and eventful day for a lazy Saturday. You were happy to see that you no longer had to get that blood thinner shot in your stomach before going to bed. You had so many bruises on your stomach because they had to pick a different spot for about ten days.

Okay, let's see how restful or eventful tomorrow will be.

Sunday, April 19, 2015
Day 16

Dear Daddy,

This morning, you were sneezing a lot. I was thinking that it was because of the plant, but I am not sure.

You said, "Today is Sunday." That made me smile. I didn't have to tell you, so that was some good progress. I also think the calendar on the wall is helping.

So I washed up today like you have been doing for the past week in the bathroom using the sink. I commend you. I will say that this is all a humbling experience.

You asked me to give you some money to count. I still had the money from the last barbershop collection. You started with the smaller bills. You struggled a little, and you were doubting yourself. It is understandable. But you are actually doing a lot better than you think.

Today was somewhat of a lazy day for us. After breakfast and a few conversations, we decided to take a nap. We had such a long week.

You had some visitors later today. Derek came by with his family to check on you, and so did your friend Outlaw. As always, Derek picked on you, and you picked on him. It's always good to see you in good spirits.

After your friends left, we decided to go outside and walk around to get some fresh air. I could tell when we were out there that you had so much on your mind. I have a lot on my mind too. I think about what will happen when your time at this facility is up. Will you ever be back to your old self? I imagine you are wondering the same thing.

When we got back in, we met another patient named Reggie. He was hit by a motorcyclist on March 18 while he was walking. Ouch. You are so good with the other patients. You find ways to make them laugh and encourage them.

After a while, you tried to send me away to do something for myself, but I didn't really feel like leaving. I am glad that I didn't. You had some more visitors.

Jerry came by. That visit had some entertaining moments. I think it is cool how you can laugh about your situation.

Jerry said to you, "Do you remember that you owe me some money?"

You thought about it for a minute, and then you said, "Naaaawww, you owe *me* money!"

Then you both started laughing.

Eventually, he tried to tell you about Uncle Melvin and the motorcycle accident. I was able to brush that off. I am so afraid of you getting razzed up and possibly having a stroke again, not sure what hearing about Uncle Melvin will do to you. Fortunately, he wasn't hurt too bad, but it's hard to explain things to you sometimes.

Steve also came by with his son. He said that he would wash your car for you. He started talking about his aunt who had recently had a stroke too, but you didn't remember her.

Anita came by. She was quiet for a little while, and then she proceeded to come out of her mouth being extra. She started getting on my nerves with her lists of "what you need to do." I was thinking, *Why don't you write it down!* I didn't want to start any drama, so I just bit my lip. She mentioned your safe deposit box at the bank, your veterans' disability money, the barbershop, blah, blah.

What was funny was that she must have irritated you too. You yelled, "Why don't you write it down! You're saying all of this stuff."

I laughed on the inside, and I could see she was probably a little embarrassed. I want to think it is all coming from a good place. I just think her delivery needs some help. She's so extra.

So my mom came by and brought me some food. It was so good. She stayed around a bit to make sure I was okay. As she was about to leave, Anita decided that she wanted to walk out with her and talk to her. About what? I didn't know at the time. She basically told Mom that you still love her. Why did she do that? See what I mean? *Extra!* I wish that she didn't do that, but Mom handled it like a champ. I always worry about her possibly being upset with conversations like that. I will save that for another exchange. But I am happy to say at the time, she was unbothered.

Anita hung around a little, but after she returned from walking and talking to my Mom, she eventually left. Goodbye!

A nurse finally brought some Afrin to you to help with your sneezing. You actually went to sleep shortly after that. It was like a power nap because when you woke up, you started talking about some of everything: the VA, your benefits, your money, and the war. Sigh. Even when we think you are sleeping, you are listening. So you heard that entire conversation, and now you are sitting there, worrying about it all. Thanks, Anita.

You eventually put your CPAP machine on, and then you were out for the night.

Monday, April 20, 2015
Day 17

Dear Daddy,

This morning, you woke up and fell back to sleep a few times. I said "good morning" to you each time. And every time after that first time, you said, "Good morning again!" You seem to get better sleep when you use that CPAP machine. The doctor wasn't kidding. You wake up so refreshed!

Joe, your occupational therapist, came to get you ready for your sessions. He said that he saw that people from the church came to see you and how nice that was. He even complimented all the pictures and messages I had posted up on your wall, saying, "It's really helpful." He then looked at you and said, "You are really into Harley, I see." You just nodded and smiled.

As I watched you interacting with Joe, I thought about all your friends and family who came by to see you. In trying to figure out what life will be like after your time at this facility, I couldn't imagine taking you away from this area and bringing you home with me to Northern Virginia. You don't really know anybody up there, and you would be miserable and unhappy. I will figure something else out.

While you were in your morning session, I called the VA. As usual, I got the runaround. I don't know why it is so hard to get anything done with them. I couldn't imagine if you had to navigate all of this. I think about the other older vets and how they are getting through all of this.

After your session, we went to the hall so you could get breakfast. It's always something there that makes me laugh. This day, in particular, was the moment when a stroke patient learned that she was getting cream of wheat for breakfast. She was not happy. She screamed, "Say what! I want some real food!" I had to hold my snicker to myself.

When you finished breakfast, you had another couple of sessions. I thought it was a good opportunity for me to run out and take care of some things. I decided to treat myself to some Waffle House. Mmmm, I love the Waffle House. After that, I went to my mom's house to take a shower. It was some much needed "me" time.

(Tip: Try to take moments away, even if it is an hour at a time. You may find yourself feeling like you can't leave for fear of something happening. Give yourself permission to get away. It doesn't have to be an extremely long amount of time. When getting away, do something that will recharge you: eat some ice cream, take a shower, sit in the park, visit somewhere there is water, and *be you*, focused on *you*. I love the Waffle House, so I enjoyed the entire time sitting there by myself, eating and drinking coffee.)

After I finished up at my mom's, I went over to your house. Oh my God! It is so extra clean. It looks really good in there. Even in the back room where you just leave laundry is straight. You have some amazing friends. Martha offered to clean your house so it could be ready for you when you come home. I was in awe! It was definitely a huge help to me for you.

I left your house on a high and with some tears of joy and relief, thinking about how supportive people have been during this time. I truly believe it is because you have made some deposits in your day, and people just want to return the favor.

When I got back to the facility, the doctor was on her way to your room. I got back just in time! When we walked in, you smiled and told me, "I can leave today." Apparently, someone told you that you were going home today. I looked at Dr. Moss for confirmation, and she just smiled and shook her head. Nice try, Dad!

Your face lit up when I told you about your house and how clean it is. Your reaction was priceless. You have such a great bunch of friends.

You got some more visitors. This time, it was Scott and Ronnie. It was a nice visit. You just kept complaining and fussing about the barbershop and how you are disappointed.

It's so nice to see how all the nurses love you so much. I guess you are a good patient. Do you remember that it was just like this at Sentara too?

You decided to give Uncle Melvin a call from your cell phone. You still don't know about his motorcycle accident, so you were surprised that he was home at that hour, but you didn't really say anything to him about it. After you two talked for a while, you handed the phone to me. Uncle Melvin was so happy to hear that you were sounding better. He still didn't want me to say anything to you about the accident. So I won't.

After the phone call, you had a few more visitors. They all had something in common with you. They all had a stroke. It was a lot of loud conversations going on in the room. I have no idea how and if you were keeping up with any of them. You just sat there and smiled, nodding occasionally.

One of the gentlemen asked me the same questions three times, and I answered it three times. He asked me about your cousin Doc and if he had been by to see you. I said no. He then told me that some people just don't want to see you like this. It has been pretty scary. You have always been invincible to me. I guess they feel the same way too.

One of the other visitors who came too was named Earl. He had a stroke too, but he didn't go to the hospital immediately. He said that he didn't have enough insurance. His left side was significantly impacted, but he's walking around and driving. His memory and speech weren't impacted at all. Then he went on to talk about what type of impact is not as bad as another. Then after thinking about it, he pretty much responded with "Six of one…" and how he didn't know which he would prefer. After a little more thought, he just said that overall, he would prefer for his mind to be right. I don't blame him for that. It's been really eye-opening, watching you in your journey to recovery.

I don't understand why when most people visit, they want to quiz you. From asking if you remember them to how you may have met them. I guess everyone just wants to be remembered.

After that round of company left, I looked around your room at the signs and messages I taped up there. I asked you if you wanted me to take them down. You didn't hear me; rather, you didn't understand me. It was like you were focused on something else. I said, "Joseph

Newby!" That got your attention. I asked you again about the stuff on the wall. You said to leave them up there in case you go crazy. Then we both started laughing. I am just glad that they were of some help during this process.

So we sat there and chatted a little. You said, "Everybody has a story. I'm blessed to have come through it. It (stroke) didn't hit me as hard as I've seen." You were right. In this facility, we are seeing so many people who are in the wheelchair because that is the only way they can get around. We are seeing people who need assistance with almost everything, from getting dressed to getting their meals. The effects of the stroke on you are not as obvious as theirs. You have your physical strength. Your speech and how you process what you hear have been impacted the most and your short-term memory.

Being that it was another beautiful day, we decided to go outside again. I will tell you that I got a serious workout pushing you in that wheelchair, especially up and down that ramp. I let you get out of the chair when we got outside since I am certified now. I just have to remember to get you back in the chair before we go back inside.

After we returned from our time outside, Anita showed up. She bought you a notepad and brought me some lipstick. Red…WTH? She kept telling me to try it. I politely declined. I really don't care for lipstick, and it's red. And why does she feel the need to push me about that? I don't get her. She tries too hard. She is a little too pushy. I can see why at times you get a little annoyed with her.

After she finished trying to get me to try on the lipstick, she proceeded to start asking you a ton of questions: What did you eat for breakfast? What did you eat for lunch? What did you eat for dinner? And then she started quizzing you. Sigh. It was painful to watch her, but hey, she's your girlfriend. I can see that you are getting annoyed with her. She just talks so much! I'm looking at her and thinking, *Why are you doing so much? Go home, lady!*

Once she finished quizzing you, I told her that I wanted to talk to her about what she said to my mom. I just didn't think it was a good move and told her to not let that happen again. You just shook your head. I think you understood some of that conversation, but you didn't say anything.

You then started to talk and told her that you love her, but you needed to relax. You also told her to only bring you stuff only when you ask. You then talked about how it is when you two travel together. "We can travel one day but without fussing."

I remember you telling me stories about how you two argue every single time you travel. I don't know how you repeatedly travel with her, to be honest with you. I've even witnessed how you two get along when we have gotten together with family for various occasions. It's…not…good.

You had more company. I am starting to wish that I kept a real log. I did have folks sign a book with messages for you, but I don't think everyone signed it.

Anita did her usual, making all the conversations ending up being about her. Tony even told me how she was telling people that I put her out of the hospital. I don't remember actually doing that even if I felt like doing it.

Finally, I got to have a side conversation with her about what she said to my mom and some other things. It was a lot of he said, she said coming from her, and she talked too much. She told my mom when she saw her that you still loved her. I really didn't appreciate that as I am protective of my mom and how she feels. I know that your marriage and divorce were a very touchy subject for her. I didn't want her to get upset. Anyway, she also told me that one of your ex-girlfriends, Sheila, told her something along the lines of me being a problem. What! I later learned that was not the case. Typical Anita, always starting shit.

After she finally left, you and I had a good conversation about when you get to go home. You told me that you wanted me to stay with you for a while. I will, Daddy. You also told me that you knew I needed to go back to work. You always say, "I don't know if you even still have a job." I do, Dad. I also appreciated that you said you understood if you needed to go back to Northern Virginia with me since I have to work. I want to do what I can to keep you on the road to recovery and avoid any repeated strokes since it is so common. I have to admit that I often worry about that and wonder if I will be able to take care of you.

Tuesday, April 21, 2015
Day 18

Dear Daddy,

We had a slightly rough start this morning. You sneezed a lot in the middle of the night.

We went to the dining room to get you some breakfast. The nurse came over to put a bib on you. I told her no and tried to politely nonverbally let her know that it was not a good idea. You almost went off. You shook your head, saying, "I don't need that thing." They call it a crumb catcher. I know you and I were both thinking about the people there who really needed it, and I think it freaked you out that they would think you needed it. On a sidenote, we know that we don't drop any food when we eat because we are greedy! So, no, ma'am, he doesn't need that.

After you finished eating, you went back to your room and laid down for a little while. So I decided to run out to get some breakfast. Yep, you guessed it, the Waffle House. I know. I know. Two days in a row. This time was a little different. I sat there and reflected and cried a little. I thought about this whole journey so far from getting the news of what happened to you to rushing down here in record speed to see you in the hospital, to staying at the hospital, to transferring to the rehabilitation center. And in the middle of all that, I thought about the emotional roller coaster of the experience. I was grateful that you have improved, and there seemed to be somewhat a light at the end of the tunnel.

After I ate breakfast, I went the VA benefits office, but no one was available because they are in training until Friday. I am just trying to figure out how to include your recent disability factored in your disability compensation.

I went to Mom's to take a shower. I know that's odd. Why didn't I go before I went to breakfast or the VA office? I don't know. I am a bit absent-minded today. When I left her house, I wondered if I even locked her door. I was on my way to Walmart to pick up some items for you, so I just turned around to go confirm that I locked the door. It was locked. Better safe than sorry. So I went to Walmart to get you some new underwear and socks. Then I stopped by your house to check on it, and man, I tell you, it is the cleanest and tidiest that I have ever seen. I called Tony and Martha to thank them. They are actually on their way to Dover Downs for the day. Good for them. They needed a break because they work so hard, and they seem to be helping so many people including us.

When I got back, I was surprised to see that you shaved your mustache off. It caught me completely off guard. You look like Lavelle, your son. It's too funny.

Today, your therapy session was a little later than usual. They checked your blood pressure, and it was a little high, so they didn't do as much as usual. I am not sure why your BP was running high today. I think the therapist startled you. They did end up giving me an update. Apparently, you are not fully cognizant of your right side. I know that the stroke damaged some of your peripheral, but I am not sure if it is permanent.

After we got back to your room, you told me that I could leave to go to the barbershop to collect your money. You actually seemed to rush me out, for some reason. I went out, collected the money, and came straight back.

Nita and Gator came by, and it was a good visit. You wanted me to help you tell them a story. It was funny because you would say parts of the story, and I would try to fill in the blanks or interpret. It felt like a game. I don't know if the story would have been funny just being told in the usual manner. But it made us all laugh.

After they left, a more "senior" nurse came in to give you your medication. You whispered to me, "Make sure she gives me the right ones." I just smiled and shook my head. She did just like the other nurses, explaining each one as she handed them to you. When she got to the last one, she said it was for your bladder. Mmm, I didn't recognize that one, for some reason, so I questioned it too, thinking about your initial request when you saw her. She double-checked it, and it was the right one, but it was for other things too. I am learning a lot about these medications. Some of them are for blood pressure, but they may help the prostate too or something that seems so on the other extreme. I have been taking so many notes.

I decided to give your brother Uncle Bernard a call on Skype. I knew that would be a funny conversation between the two of you. You are always picking on each other. He kept asking you questions to see what you remember. "Since you think you know so much, what's your address?" You would give him a silly stare. Good comic relief.

After that, I called Mike on Skype too. You really like him. I am glad that you do.

By the end of the evening, when it was almost time to go to bed, you actually asked for the CPAP machine. I guess you are actually feeling some of the benefits of using it. I hear that it helps you get some really good sleep. It may be a little awkward at first, but they say it will help with your blood pressure if you are getting good rest. That sleep apnea is so scary. I still think about being in the ICU with you and freaking out the first time I heard those alarms ringing to indicate that you stopped breathing momentarily. That messed my nerves up! The CPAP is supposed to help with that.

Wednesday, April 22, 2015
Day 19

Dear Daddy,

Around midnight, the nurses came in as usual to check your vitals. I still don't understand why it is so late, but I guess they have to still keep a watch on you since the risk of having a repeated stroke is so great after the first one. They check your blood every few days to see if your clotting medication has kicked in. I think they startled you a little, asking you the traditional questions like "What's your name, Mr. Newby?" Okay, I am just kidding, but that did happen one time. Okay, back to the questions: "What's your name?" and "When's your birthday?" You answered "Newby Joseph" and gave your birthday.

Nurse Peggy commented that you are doing way better than when you got there. One of the nurses was checking your blood pressure, and the other was drawing blood. I think the one taking your blood pressure did something incorrectly because she had to do it again. Thankfully, the one who was drawing blood got it right the first time.

I can't seem to go back to sleep. It is about 1:00 a.m. I said a prayer and thought about today and that your discharge is going to be in a few days. Should we do some sort of welcome home party? I don't know. I keep thinking of you being somewhat fragile. I don't want the risk of you falling ill again.

I started thinking about arrangements for when I have to leave you to return to Northern Virginia. Are you going to stay here or are you going home with me? Would it be okay for Uncle Clifton to stay with you for a little while during your recovery? I immediately hear the "hell no" reaction you had when he asked you that a few weeks ago.

Finally, I fell back to sleep.

It's Meghan's birthday. I thought it would be a good idea to call her on Skype to sing "Happy Birthday." I knew she would love that, even if we didn't sing it right. Seeing you singing and laughing made her day. She even cried a little.

Sigh, Anita called, trying to be helpful again. She said something about Michael Douglas hiring the best speech therapist and maybe that's what "we" can do. Interesting how she says "we." Well, you were in the bathroom when she called, so I told her that you would call her later.

One of the patients we met, Mr. Minga (Kyle), is leaving. He was tearing up when he was saying goodbye to the nurses. It was very hard and emotional. I can't recall how long he had been in this facility, but you seem to form some interesting bonds here, and you make a lot of connections.

I called Anita back for you, and you talked to her for a few minutes.

After you got off the phone, the nurses came in to take your blood pressure. It was up a little. I asked them to take it again. You closed your eyes and took a deep breath, and the next check came in lower. Whew...I know. It makes me nervous too.

Today, you had an extra speech therapy session, and I got certified to take you outside *without* the wheelchair! Yes! I don't have to push you up and down those inclines anymore. So we went outside for a few.

As soon as you got outside, you spotted your Benz parked on the street, and you fussed a little, but there were no regular spaces left at the facility. It's funny how you immediately noticed that.

We didn't stay too long because I knew some more people were coming to see you. After we got back to your room, Hartwell and Tyronne came by. They were pleased to see you. Of course, the nurses would show up to check your pressure. And it was high. Everyone in the room raised their eyebrows except for me and the nurses. I figured it was because you were excited.

After your company left, we went outside again. It's so much easier without having to deal with that wheelchair! We went to the first-floor lobby and decided to go sit on the patio. It was some good daddy-daughter time. You talked about what you were going to eat as your first meal outside. You wanted steak, for some reason. I have no idea why. I told you I wanted seafood. I am sure that we will find a place that will accommodate both of us. We will figure it out.

Your friend Ronnie came back to visit. I think he has diabetes. His visits always seem to depress me a little. He's always going down the list of people who are sick or have died. At the end of the conversation, it seems to get somewhat positive…I think.

We have some interesting conversations when it is just you and me. You talked about how the nurses give you a shower and how you used to be shy, but you figured you are paying them, so they might as well clean you up.

Your friend Charlene came to see you. She said that she went to the barbershop since you can't cut her hair. You said, "You wouldn't have paid me. That's what broke me!" She looked at you shocked and then started laughing. I guess she is one of your folks who gets the hook up.

While she was there, she mentioned your friend Fat Ricks and how he had passed away. I didn't know who he was to inform you about him, but I do recall learning that he was actually in Sentara the same time as you were right after you had your stroke. You were surprised and saddened a little. But somehow, I can see how you thought about yourself and how you are fortunate and making it through.

Nurses came in to check your blood pressure, and it was high. They decided to take you off the Claritin because your blood pressure was more important than the sinus issues.

Doc arrived. I guess he had been by before, but every time he came, you were in therapy. Dang, now I feel bad about my response to the other guy. But technically, I didn't see him come by…oh well.

Doc suggested that I send you to the VA for further rehabilitation as opposed to trying to take care of you myself. I don't want to do that to you. It's like putting you in a home. Plus, you have been counting down the days to when you can leave this facility, to only take you to another one.

Your friend Gwynn came to see you. He asked me about Anita. We actually had a whole conversation about her without any words. The facial expressions said a lot. In so many words, he said that she is a piece of work. I agree.

Yvonne's brother came by. It's wild how he looks just like her.

You keep telling everyone about the showers and how they keep the door open. It's funny to me every time I hear about it, and everyone laughs when they hear it too. I guess the idea of some women, well, the nurses who are women, giving you a shower. Pretty much washing you like a car.

After everyone left, we sat around for a while. You asked me to refill your water container. Wow. You are asking for it now. Before, I would have to remind you to drink some water. I love it. That's all I drank the whole time here with you, and my skin looks amazing. I lost a lot of weight, but I think that is because of the stress.

I asked you to edge my hairline on my neck. I thought it would feel good for you to do something you're naturally good at doing. As you were cutting my hair, you were complaining about the clippers. "These tools ain't worth a damn." I snickered without moving my head so you wouldn't slip and mess up my hairline.

After you finished with my hair, the nurse came to get you for your shower. You were gone for like twenty minutes, and when you got back, the nurse asked me if you have a barbershop. She said that her boyfriend goes to the shop, and my cousin cuts his hair. Small world.

As we settled down for the evening, we talked about you not being able to live alone and how I have to manage everything. I think you misunderstood my acknowledgement of it because you looked at me and said, "I don't think you know how serious this is."

I nodded my head and said, "I do."

You mentioned that your arm was tingling. Of course, that made me nervous. I am starting to think about what it will be like when you are at home alone. I am a little scared to leave you alone.

That night, I talked to Mike, my boyfriend, and I asked him to come down when you are discharged and stay with us for at least the first night. I know you like him a lot, and it will be good to have a man there for your firsts back at home. I don't know if I will be able to handle everything by myself.

Still worried about that arm tingling, I asked the nurses to come by to check on you. Fortunately, your blood pressure is good. Everything is good. I am getting nervous as we get closer to you being home.

Thursday, April 23, 2015
Day 20

Dear Daddy,

You woke up early today. "Good morning, good morning. I have to pee!" At least, you are following the rules about getting out of bed. That alarm will still sound off if you get up on your own.

I am just relieved to see that you are okay.

You mentioned that in your sleep, you heard "God is good" over and over again. You realized that was all you had to say, and it didn't have to be anything extravagant.

You talked about the nurses coming in to check on you. You said you were asleep, but you could see them, and you asked me if I saw them. I haven't been able to sleep too well since your stroke, so yes, I saw them.

I reminded you that you are going home tomorrow. You said, "I know, I kept you a long time." I think you meant they kept you a long time. Your tone came across as if you will believe it when you see it. It's funny how a week ago, you kept asking if you were going home tomorrow. I guess eventually, you gave up on that.

We had another deep conversation today. You said, "God touched me." And you told me that was why you liked to go outside to look at the trees and the water. I felt a tear forming in my eye, but I didn't let it fall.

You said, "It's seven o'clock!" I looked at you and smiled. Progress. You got it right the first time!

I started smelling something. I looked at you and asked, "Dad, did you fart?" You gave me a blank look, so I said, "Poot?"

You just looked at me and laughed a little and said, "I did it for one second."

I could only shake my head.

Anita called, talking your head off as usual. I still don't think that she is good for you. What's interesting is that I think you may be realizing that too.

After that, you did the usual breakfast, and then you had your last speech therapy session for your time at this facility. You've made significant improvement, but you have ways to go.

The care coordinator came by to talk to me about you doing more speech therapy after you are discharged. So I will get you on the schedule.

While waiting for you to finish your therapy session, I have been working on your VA disability stuff. It is so complicated, but I thank God that I can get a lot done online. It works out so much easier than running around and shuffling papers. It's still a bit frustrating as I continue to think about if you had to navigate all of this on your own. What about others in your situation who may not have the help they need? It makes me sad.

After your therapy session, Anita showed up. Thankfully, your friend Bobby Lane came by too. I love having someone to offset her. She's draining. Bobby Lane was talking to you about vitamins, and I guess the word didn't sound right to you so you kept repeating it with a confused look, "Vitamins! Vitamins?"

And of course, you shared your story about your shower experience. I don't think it will ever get old.

Another one of your friends came by named Yvonne. Her arm was in a sling. She was in a car accident. In sharing her story, she started preaching. You then told her that God is good, and you learned how good He is.

Noticing that the room was starting to get a little crowded, Bobby Lane left, and shortly, Yvonne left too.

Your friend Spratley came by; he's Uncle Melvin's brother by adoption. His visit was a little gloomy to me. He talked about some child passing away. I was on Skype with Mike (my boyfriend) and was passively paying attention to that conversation. I could see your face. So I asked to change the conversation. I don't think you knew what he said, but you could tell it wasn't good, so you started to worry a little.

After everyone finally left, you laid down. Judy, one of our ex-girlfriends, called me. When you realized who it was, you wanted to say hi. It was a short conversation, but you did get to say hello.

You asked me about Dennis, and you wanted to know how he was doing since you heard that he had a few repeated strokes. I talked to his wife, and it sounds like he is making good progress too.

Before the night was over, the nurses came in to check your blood pressure, and it was a little high, but they weren't alarmed. They gave you your nightly dose of your medication.

I am really excited about you getting to go home finally. I am going to be here for the next few weeks to help you get adjusted and close to being back to normal, whatever that looks like now.

Friday, April 24, 2015
Day 21

Dear Daddy,

You are going home today! You are so excited. You told me that you could hear me talking all night. I was on the phone with Mike.

As you were getting ready, the nurses and many of the therapists came to give you a hug. They really liked you. You were actually a really good patient.

Nurse John will be checking you out, going over all the procedures and stuff with me. It's funny; he's the one who checked you in, so it was full circle. I tried to explain that to you, but you couldn't fully process what I was saying, and I guess I wasn't patient enough to keep trying, so you got a little frustrated. I then just told you that it wasn't important.

We went to eat breakfast in the dining room for the last time. You ate pretty quickly. I guess you are really ready to go!

We went back to your room, and you continued to pack your stuff. You started taking the cards and stuff off the wall. You said it was sentimental. I took a picture of you standing proud in front of the makeshift calendar I put on your wall.

While you were packing, your cousin Junkyard came by. Apparently, he had a similar stroke in 2012. He asked if you remembered him. You did. I didn't. But what matters is that you remembered him. He didn't stay too long because he came with a friend of his. His friend got a call, and they left. And wildly enough, the alarms started going off in the building. Someone had just died who is upstairs. I don't know if that was connected or not.

You said, "Wow, it's a lot of people who got sick." I just agreed with you. I could only sit there and be thankful that you are recovering.

When it was time to go, I had to sit down with Nurse John to go over all the instructions. It was a big purple binder. You looked at me, and I looked at you. I guess we were both wondering, *What in the world?* Nurse John opened the binder and went over each page and discussed your medications, the schedule, what to do if your blood pressure gets too high, what to do if you have another stroke, etc. Even as I write this, I start getting overwhelmed. Each time he turned the page and started talking, I would look at you, and you would look at me as to say, "Are you sure you got all that?" I would just look at you and nod. In my mind, I was saying, *Oh my God, I don't know if I can do this.* There were so many things to do. I even had to go get your prescriptions, but I had to confirm what you had at home first.

Finally, we have finished the discharge paperwork. Nurse John came back with a wheelchair for you to be rolled out of the building. It was part of their protocol. Of course, you questioned it for a second, then you just got in the chair. One of the CNAs ended up wheeling you out of the facility. You waved and said bye to everyone. You were like a rock star rolling through there. One of the nurses said that you were one of her favorites. The nurse assistant who wheeled you out also helped you get in the passenger seat of the truck. I made sure I drove your Harley truck today. I thought it would be easier to get in since it was higher than the car. I buckled you up, and then we left.

It was a little after lunchtime when we finally left, so I asked you if you wanted to get something to eat. You wanted Golden Corral. Okay, that was easy. We went to Golden Corral, and you made your hefty plate. While you were sitting down, you looked so happy to be out and about. It was really obvious when you started recognizing people in there. You were smiling and yelling, "Hey!" And of course, people would come say hi, and they would say they were happy to see that you were okay. I would explain what you couldn't when asked.

After lunch, we finally went to your house. Martha and Tony were there waiting on you. It was a good welcome. You were so shocked at how clean your house was. Martha did some wonderful organizing of your things with various containers and such.

They stayed for a little while, and then they left. It was just you and me. So I decided to flip through that binder and start figuring out what I needed to do about your medication. I then started organizing your current meds to determine which prescriptions I needed to get filled. I opened a bottle that I thought was your blood thinner. It said "warfarin," and it included a description of the pill. It said it was a small pink pill. Well, the pills in the bottle were blue. Hmmm…what are these? I asked you. You got on the defensive and told me that I shouldn't be messing with your stuff. I told you how I wanted to make sure that you were taking the right medicine at the right time. Then after us going back and forth for a while, you said it was Viagra. You actually said that were your "f" pills. You actually said the whole word. I wanted to at least write that on the bottle, but you insisted that I didn't need to mess with it. Then you said, "I don't know why you have to even mess with them!" I just wanted to make sure you took the right stuff. I put them in your room. I was tired.

Shortly after this, Karen came by to see you. I was glad. She could keep you distracted for a few.

Bringing you home felt like bringing home a newborn baby who could cuss. I started getting really irritated with you and this whole situation. I walked outside to call Mike. I started crying and told him that I didn't think I could do this. He said he was sorry that I was going through this, and he asked me what he could do to make me feel better. I told him, "Nothing!" Then I asked how far he was because I needed help. He wasn't too far away.

I went back in the house to continue to figure out what I needed to do. Mike finally showed up, and I almost started crying again. He told me to come outside to help me calm down. We went outside for a few minutes, and I got myself together. He said that he would go with me to go get the prescriptions and whatever I needed to get. I had to go back in the house to get some things first.

As I was in the house getting my stuff together to go run errands, I heard Mike say, "Mr. Newby, I want to ask your daughter if she would do the honor of marrying me?" He had the ring in his hand, and I looked back at him like "What are you doing?" And, Dad, you were screaming, "Are you serious!" Even Karen was screaming that too. Then I realized that he wasn't joking, and I started tearing up again. He said, "So will you marry me?" I nodded and started crying, and then I cried on his shoulder. The picture proves that I had a rough day. My eyes looked terrible!

You and Karen were both crying, and then you both commented on how beautiful the ring was.

After about what seemed like a few minutes, we proceeded to go run these errands. When I got in the car, I got to take a really good look at my finger. It was beautiful.

We got the medications you needed and returned home.

Mike stayed with us as I requested because I was still nervous about you being home. What if you have another stroke? What if your blood pressure spikes? What if you stop breathing? I was just so scared of what could possibly happen now since we didn't have the security of nurses.

Saturday, April 25, 2015
Day 22

Dear Daddy,

Today was a pretty low-key day. I slept somewhat okay last night, but I felt like I had to come in and check on your ever so often. I got so used to the nurses coming in and checking on you. Now I would just open your door and make sure I hear you snoring or something. You are sleeping with your CPAP machine, so that's good. Mike understood me wanting to check on you frequently. I am a bit paranoid. I guess I keep worrying about something happening, and I don't know what to do or, even worse, you not waking up. I think I ended up with a few hours of sleep.

As I was saying, it was a pretty low-key day.

We spent the day just letting you get acclimated to being home. I would give you your medication on the scheduled intervals.

Today was also Mike's birthday. Interesting. I think it would be easy for us both to remember the exact date we got engaged. I digress.

So we went to Surf Riders for dinner. You love this place. We like it too. While we were eating, you looked at my ring and said, "Boy, that's a big ring! Mike, you did good!" And then you laughed.

After dinner, we went back to your house. You said that you wanted to go to church tomorrow. You decided to pull out what you were going to wear, pulling out a few neckties and showing Mike. Then you pulled out some of your cowboy boots. You have a really nice collection of the different kinds and colors. Mike complimented one of my favorite ones you have, those blue, eel-skinned ones. He had a blue suit that he planned on wearing to church, and you told him that he could wear your boots. I didn't realize that you two have the same shoe size. You two have a lot in common. Now I can add the love of shoes and your shoe size.

To finish your outfit for church, you were trying on different neckties. Mike commented on how he struggles with tying them. You said, "Oh, it's easy." And then you proceeded to just tie it and make a nice knot in seconds like it was nothing. Then you did it again to show Mike how to do it. We were both impressed. I was just happy to see that you remembered it so easily. I just watched in awe.

    We called it a night since we had church in the morning. Anita will be coming with us. Pray for me.

Sunday, April 26, 2015
Day 23

Dear Daddy,

    This morning was pretty interesting. As we were getting ready, when it was time for you to tie your necktie, you couldn't remember how to do it. I couldn't believe it. I don't know what happened. Maybe you were just excited. You got so frustrated. You even started looking worried. I kept thinking of how you had tied several ties last night. And I guess you were thinking the same thing. Mike got you to calm down, and he ended up tying the tie for you. "It won't be as fancy as yours, but this will be okay." Another moment I wondered what I would have done if Mike wasn't there. I don't even know how to tie a tie. I guess you would have gone without it? I don't know.

    Anita got to the house right before it was time for us to leave to go to church.

    It was nice to go with you to church, especially after the ordeal we experienced. We are so grateful to God that you survived and did not have a repeat episode. I am grateful that I am able to be here with you.

    During a part of the praise and worship, you felt moved and opened your arms and looked up. And then you walked up to the front of the church. I followed you up there. We both had tears in our eyes. We hugged, and without words, we both shared a whole conversation on gratitude. Mike and Anita had tears in their eyes too when we returned to our seats.

    You even got a shout out from Pastor Riddick. Everyone clapped when he mentioned your name and what you experienced.

    After the church service, you wanted to go to the Piccadilly, a local cafeteria-style restaurant. I was happy with that choice because I love their carrot soufflé. Fortunately, when we got there, there wasn't a line. We were able to go straight to the food line to pick out our meal options.

You're still not as comfortable ordering food at restaurants. It's only been a few days, so that is to be expected. I thought that you would want Anita to help you pick out your food. You said, "No, Anita can't pick my food. I want you to do it." I guess you are so used to me looking out for you. Plus, you know she will try to make you get some items you don't want. So I picked your food. I don't think Anita liked that too much.

After we ate, we hung out for a little at your house. Mike had to leave to go back to Northern Virginia. I was sad to see him go for multiple reasons, including being a little nervous about being home by myself with you. Do I know what to do if anything happens?

We sat on the porch for a little while. Some of your friends came by to see you. We got the unfortunate news that Sassy, a lady motorcycle buddy whom even I admired, had committed suicide. What? She was so tough. I remember meeting her, and she had this vicious motorcycle that was so loud. I wanted to be like her. She even did a cross-country motorcycle ride by herself. Apparently, the trip was a very eventful one that took her through a lot of emotions. I could only imagine. I don't know what made her feel the need to end her life, and I don't think I will ever know. Of course, it took a little bit to get the dots connected for you to remember who she was. You were shocked too.

After your friends left, you asked me how you sound to people. I told you that it was definitely different, but you always spoke fast. People actually joke about that. You still struggle finding the right words, but I think people are understanding. At least, I think they are. They may be just waiting for you to make a complete recovery.

Anita wanted to spend the night tonight. You asked her if she was spending the night, and she said, "Whatever you want, Jojo." Sigh. I have never in my whole life heard anyone call you "Jojo." But okay. What she didn't get, or maybe she did, is that you wanted her to say yes or no.

She ended up spending the night.

Monday, April 27, 2015
Day 24

Dear Daddy,

Out of habit, I slept with my door partially opened. Why did I do that?

You got up and walked out of your room, and I don't think you had any underwear on. Then shortly after, she walked out of the room like that too. What in the world? Did you both forget that I was here?

When you both went back in the room, I got up to fix some breakfast. I made some Turkey bacon and egg and cheese sandwiches. You always eat pork bacon, so I wanted to try to let you take a break from that. I am not sure how much that will help, but it doesn't hurt anything.

Anita made her way back into the kitchen. She talks *way* too much. She felt the need to tell me that you tried to get some. She said you told her that "it still works." And then she shook her head laughing. Why does she feel so inclined to share this? I don't know.

After breakfast, since you had company, I decided it was a good opportunity to run some errands. Your truck needed an oil change. They mentioned that you needed some other work too, but I opted to just let them change the oil. We will address the other stuff later.

Apparently, Anita took you out for lunch and for a pedicure. I tried to call both your number and hers. No answer. Why wasn't her phone on? I really didn't like that I couldn't reach you to see that you were okay.

You guys finally got back to the house. You were okay.

Some of your good friends came to see you. They were surprised that you were out and about. I guess they thought you would be in the house or maybe even in the bed. I was told that they stayed away because of me. Hmmm…I do remember shutting down your visitation when you were in ICU. Oh well, whatever.

While you had your company, I worked through my action list. I called your attorney about your accident from last year. Looks like the other driver didn't have any insurance, so your insurance will be paying you. When it is all said and done, you may end up with four thousand dollars. This is unfortunate. I don't know why you decided to get an attorney. I realized in the conversation that the lawyer was going to end up getting a higher piece of the settlement than you. I voiced this to him on the phone. I think he will see what he can do to shift some of those dollars because that makes no sense. And that is actually what I told him. "How does it sound that your client is ending up with less than you and the firm?" I said it politely, and that may have helped.

My next call was about some IRA you set up. I was trying to see if you could get the whole amount or did it have to be distributed periodically. Well, it looks like you did something that will not allow you to draw from it all at once. You will get it once per year for the next ten years. I guess you forgot?

Your company left. I think that's good. You need a break anyway.

I decided to tackle the bucket of mail. Oh my. It was so much in there. I am so glad that I at least got your accounts set up some years back for online payments. It's funny. Three years ago, I had no idea that I would need to completely manage your bills. I just got it set up for when you would ask me to pay bills for you on occasion as opposed to writing out paper checks all the time.

After finishing up the mail, we decided to do some of your therapy activities. You wanted to go over your numbers. I imagined that I would want to do that too so I could count money! I wonder if that was why you wanted to focus on that. It's cute to see you using your fingers to count and remember the numbers. I am just happy to see you progressing.

When we finished your numbers activity, I changed your blood pressure medication patch. I am wondering if I should have done it sooner. I'm still a little nervous, but you seem to be doing okay with how I am doing things.

Tuesday, April 28, 2015
Day 25

Dear Daddy,

We got up early and had breakfast.

Your blood pressure was a little high this morning. It was at the level that the nurse said to give you the clonidine tablet to bring it down a bit. I gave you one, and we checked your blood pressure shortly after. You were good to go.

You had your first speech therapy session since leaving the rehabilitation facility. This was pretty big since you weren't technically being forced to do it. Well, you were. Because I was not letting you ease off the gas yet. It was a good session. This was really just to assess where you are and let the therapist devise a plan based on where you are. This session wore you out, but it was a good one. I was really impressed with this therapist.

My highlight for this session was when she was showing you flashcards. You remembered most of them. But when she showed you one with a squirrel on it, you paused. You said, "Hmm, I don't remember what it's called, but I eat them."

The therapist's eyes got wide open. She said, "You eat squirrels!"

I could only smile and whisper to her that you like to hunt, like that would make her feel better. It didn't, but it was so funny. We will laugh about this forever.

After therapy, we went to visit your barbershop. Everyone was so happy to see you, and I could tell that you felt good going in there, even if it was just to sit and watch people. There was a gentleman there who gave you a pep talk, and then he ended up singing an encouraging song to you. I recorded it. I don't think you fully understood what he was saying to you, but you knew it was something good.

We left the shop and rode around a little. We stopped by my Uncle John's house (my mom's brother), but he wasn't home. The community center that you used to go to before your stroke was on our route, and it was open. You wanted to stop by. There were some people in there playing cards, and there was a fitness facility in there. I didn't know you went there. The people at the table playing cards were so happy to see you. I helped you tell them that you had a stroke, and you just got out of the hospital. They were shocked, but they said you looked good. They told you to come back to play cards with them.

It was a pretty busy morning. We headed back to your house. When we got there, you decided to sit on the porch. I went in the house to make some phone calls. I could hear you whistling while sitting out there. It was cute. I guess you were just glad to be home.

I called my temporary replacement back at my job, Andy. He told me how impressed he was at the volume of work and products and how I made it look a lot easier than it really was. It felt good to hear that since I had felt like I was being taken for granted at work. There were a few things that happened before your stroke that confirmed that for me, but I don't want to worry you with that. I know that overall, I will be okay.

You got a few visitors while I was on the phone, but they didn't stay too long.

You came back in to watch some television. You have a hard time keeping up with it. The riots in Maryland after the death of Freddie Gray have been playing on a lot of the channels. Without fully understanding what's going on, it can be pretty stressful and frustrating to watch. Well, damn, having an understanding of what's going on can make you feel uneasy too. It's hard to believe what's still going on in the world. What's going on right here at home.

You asked for your phone today. I had offered it to you a few days ago, but you didn't seem interested. Now you were ready for it. I got some bad news for you. It was wiped. I tried to unlock it, and when you had your stroke, you couldn't remember how to unlock it. You couldn't remember your code or pattern to unlock it. You have an android phone. I am team iPhone. I don't really know too much on using your android even though you would always ask me to help you with it. The good news was that I was able to back up you contacts to the cloud somehow. How? I do not even remember.

First person you wanted to call was Anita. What was funny was that you really didn't feel like talking to her or maybe she wore you out in the conversation so quickly. After you ended the call, you handed the phone back to me and asked me to keep it until later.

You took a quick nap in your favorite chair, and when you woke up, you wanted some of the leftovers from Surf Riders. When we checked your blood pressure and it was running somewhat high, you changed your mind. So I ate it instead. LOL.

Instead of giving you that medicine to quickly lower your blood pressure, I decided to wait a bit to see if it would come down on its own. I am so leery of giving you extra medication. I feel like you take so much already. I decided to get us out to take a walk on your street to get some fresh air and some exercise.

When we got back from our walk, you took your evening medication. I guess now I know that I can at least wait a bit to see what naturally will happen. I still think about if your blood pressure reaches that level it was when you had a stroke.

I am really looking forward to taking you up to New Jersey to see your mom, my grandmother, Nanny. She and the rest of the family have been worried about you. I have been keeping them up to date via group texts. Looking back on that, I think I have some ideas on how to keep people better informed. The different group messages were a little overwhelming. If I had to tell someone how to do it for their loved one, maybe I would say use an app like GroupMe or WhatsApp and then add folks to the thread as appropriate, and people can leave when they want.

So we will be heading to New Jersey after we stop at my house in Northern Virginia for my birthday.

My mom called. She wanted to talk about how you were doing. I was a little stressed today, and my fuse was short, so I didn't really feel like going into detail. I was probably a bit rude to her. I think she understands. She had to be a caregiver for her mom some years ago. She knows the potential stress the caregiver can have. I am thankful that she does understand.

Mike called to check in on us. It is always nice to hear how you two talk to each other. He said that he will be going to New Jersey with us. That's good. It will be nice to have him there to help.

Ronald called. He was so thrilled to hear that you sound better than you did the last time he saw you. You called him by his nickname as opposed to calling him his brother's name. That made him feel good. You had a good conversation with him.

At the end of the day, we had one of our usual conversations where you started remembering bits and pieces of what you experienced the day you had the stroke. You asked me, "How did they get in my head to fix it? I had no surgery?" I didn't get to you until a few hours after your stroke, and you were at the hospital. I only know they administered something that was supposed to help, but it had to be done as soon as possible. The earlier the better.

We called it a night after that. I'm so tired.

Tuesday, April 28, 2015
Day 25

Dear Daddy,

 This morning, I woke up and picked up your house phone. I realized that I hadn't looked at it since we came back to your house. I started clearing out the caller ID, and your phone made a loud, odd sound with each deletion. You heard me and said, "What's that?" You were a bit concerned. Your eyes were closed and squinting. I showed you what it was, and then you were okay.

 I decided to play some jazz to relax your mind a little. You said it was a good idea.

 Tip: I read some articles online about how it is good for people with brain injuries to listen to music without any words, like classical or jazz. Consider having it playing in the morning. It can help with starting the day off on a positive note. Your loved one is already tense because nothing is normal to them anymore. This is one gesture to help them relax. Without words, they can just pay attention to the melody. My dad actually started humming what he heard when he caught the pattern.

 I cooked some oatmeal this morning. I figured it would be good for you since it helps with cholesterol. You are actually taking a medication for it, so why not?

 When you tried it, as politely as possible, let me know that you don't like it. You ate it, though. It held you all day, and it surprised you. You even told your friends about it later. I guess you couldn't believe it.

 Later in the day, we went to the credit union to check your safe deposit box. Apparently, you have some coins in there. Anita has you thinking that they are some high-dollar coins and that it would be safer for them to be placed in a safe deposit box. Shoot, I was curious then.

 When we got there, we showed your ID and the key, and they let us back there to open your box. It was those collectors of President

Barack Obama coins that you see on TV. They were gold. Um, well, they are special, but they aren't worth nearly as much as Anita led you to believe. God bless Anita. That's all I can say. You were adamant that they are valuable and that they needed to stay there. So they stayed there.

We left just in time to make it to you doctor's appointment at the VA. You were dreading this appointment. You kept saying, "She told me this would happen." And then you would shake your head. And you were right. Dr. T. said that she told you right before your stroke that if you didn't take your medication, change some of your habits, and lose some weight, you will have a stroke. You sat there and listened to her and said, "I know."

I was sitting there, thinking, *Wow, she's tough, but she's good!* I couldn't believe that I had no idea about your health. I guess you felt you had it all under control, so I didn't need to know. I didn't even know you were prescribed most of the medication you are on now a while back. You just weren't taking them correctly, if at all. It got me thinking. It's a lot of different medications, all with varying schedules: one med you are supposed to take twice per day, another med only at midday, one med only at night, another med half of the pill at night, and another med only if your blood pressure reaches a certain level. Your patch has to be changed weekly. It's funny that I can remember that, but I have all my memory. I will put together a solution in bit.

After we left the VA, you mentioned that you wanted to have some spaghetti today. I can make that.

We stopped by mom's house since it was on the way. Her brother, my Uncle Ernest, was there. You said, "Oh, I thought he was dead." I have no idea why you thought that, but he's alive and kicking. We did a quick visit there, and then we tried Uncle John's house again. They were actually eating spaghetti and offered us some. We declined. That oatmeal really did hold you for a long time during the day. You were still full from that.

After leaving there, we stopped at one of your best friend's house, Lip. Some of your mutual friends were there. They were all happy to see you. Some of them kept commenting how I shut down your visitation at the hospital. They even said that I did the right thing. For the few who gave me a hard time for that decision, there were many more who praised that move. I would do it again if I had to go back and do it all over.

We left Lip's house and went to the grocery store to get some items for our spaghetti dinner. You saw a little baby with his mother, and you handed him a five-dollar bill. You said, "Is this okay? Something told me to give it to him." The mother nodded and said "thank you." You smiled. I decided to buy some lottery tickets. I wish something would tell you the winning numbers. But hey, you never know.

When we got home, I cooked the spaghetti. I decided to make it with ground turkey and whole wheat pasta. I am trying different ways to give you some healthier alternatives. It came out pretty good. You liked it. I told you it was turkey, and you were surprised. You said that when Anita cooked with turkey, it didn't taste like that. I don't know. It might be in how she seasoned it. Needless to say, you are now okay with eating ground turkey.

Some of your friends came by while you were eating. They were admiring your plate. I offered them some, but they said it was okay. They stayed for a little while and then left. After they left, you asked for seconds. Score!

After eating, I started thinking about your medication and what to do about it. I took a picture of each of your medications and their bottle. I sent the photos to the local drug store to get them developed.

I decided to run to the drug store to pick up the photos and a few other items. I got you a few pill organizers, the ones that have four parts to the day. It was perfect because your prescription schedule was hokey like that. I got some labels to put "morning," "2:00 p.m.," "evening," and "bedtime" on each day of the week. Perfect. I think the container has morning, midmorning, afternoon, and bedtime.

When I got home, I started working on the labels and putting them on the organizer. I then went through your medication in the bottles to start dropping them in their designated slots. I don't know why I think about what if I was not here. I wondered who would be able to refill these correctly. So I decided to write down your schedule on a piece of paper so anyone could come in and refill when necessary. They would have the list and the photos.

Tip: Try to prepare things like someone is going to help you even when it doesn't look like it will happen. You never know who you will need to call in a pinch. Getting a pill organizer helps significantly if there are multiple prescriptions.

It was helpful to have them organized instead of fuddling with those multiple pill bottles and their unique times.

May 7, 2015

Dear Daddy,

It's my birthday, and we are spending time at my house. It was wild returning home to Northern Virginia. You could tell that my life literally stopped when I left. I was supposed to be a bridesmaid. There were some dishes in the sink. It just looked like life had paused.

Mike, Kayla, and my mom came to the house too. We all ended up going to dinner at Sakura, a Japanese steak house. Actually, one of my favorites. It was nice. You were on my right side and my mom on the other. I never thought that would happen again until another life milestone. I guess the wedding, maybe?

Dinner was cool. We enjoyed being entertained while our meal was being prepared. Mike treated us all to dinner for my birthday. We ended up taking some pictures.

When we got back to my house, Mike surprised me with a birthday cake with a picture of my Harley on it. It was so cool. I was so surprised to see it. So thoughtful. I remember him asking me for a picture of the bike a little while back, but I didn't know why or some excuse he gave me made sense, I guess.

After we ate cake, you wanted my iPad to do some exercises. I opened it, and then you started going through them. You looked at Kayla, and she could tell you were wanting some help with it. You told her she was smart. So she helped you. What was amazing while this was going on was my mom and how she watched you struggle with simple words. She was at a loss for words. It seems like it was at that moment that she finally forgave you for the time you were together and divorced. She let go. She said, "Wow, I had no idea it was this bad, Shaunté." I just nodded. The thirty plus years of pain and resentment she had been carrying seemed to just go away at that instant.

May 12, 2015

Dear Daddy,

It looks like you are getting tired of getting up to go to the therapy session. I had an idea that you weren't too happy with them being in the morning, so I rescheduled them to later in the day. I just thought in the beginning, we would try to follow a similar schedule to what you had at the facility. You told me that you really didn't want to go, and you wanted to relax to see what you could do on your own. I don't think that's a good idea. You still have a couple of weeks scheduled.

Later this afternoon, I thought about how I could get you to be even more self-sufficient with your medication. Your phone. I put four different alarms in your phone and titled them by your medication. I started the first one this evening.

I proceeded to explain and show you your medication, pointing out the different parts of the day. I told you that your phone will let you know when it is time to take each one instead of me telling you all day. You seemed to like it. You looked at the container to get your bearings.

When the alarm went off, I handed you the container. You got your evening medication out and took it.

A few hours later, the next alarm went off for your bedtime medication. You got up and took it.

I think this may be a good move.

May 13, 2015

Dear Daddy,

    Interesting day. I guess it was a rollover from last night. You have been fussing at me a lot lately.

    The alarm that I put on your phone for medicine worked out well. It went off at 8:00 a.m., and you jumped up, saying, "Good idea." You walked up front in your underwear to find your medicine dispenser. You actually found the Thursday morning dosage with no issues. You took your pills, and then you went to lay back down. I tried to get you to get up and get ready, but you wanted to lay down to sleep for a few minutes. I decided to let you and continued getting ready.

    I was on the phone when I heard you rush to get up only after lying down for a few minutes. You wanted to make your breakfast drink. You started looking for some apples, and I told you that I threw them away last night because we had them so long. You said, "Apples don't go bad." I just stayed silent because it's so easy to argue with you these days. Then you just stood there in your underwear, looking around, trying to get your bearings. I started pulling out the ingredients for you. You poured everything in there and made your shake. I was proud of you. It was a little dramatic, but you got it done.

    So I asked you to go take your shower. You complained about it being early, but you took it. After you got dressed, you started complaining again about the speech therapy and how you don't feel it's worth your time. You feel that you should be able to take time to heal naturally. I let you share your frustrations, and then we went to therapy.

    On the porch this afternoon, we were talking about your heartbeat being irregular. You asked me if they were going to do anything, like shocking you, to make your heart beat regularly. I shook my head. You agreed, and in so many words, you said that it'd been like that all your life, so there was no need to change it. Then I asked what you wanted to do if something happened to you. I made the "passing out" gesture and the electric shock gesture. You screamed, "Oh yes! By all means!" We laughed. Your reaction was funny.

You expressed the fact that you could drive. You went on and on about you being able to drive, but you didn't want to. I think you know the mechanics, but I'm not sure of your reaction time. It was only a few days ago that you didn't even know how to operate the power windows. But okay.

I will say that I feel tired. It gets challenging with you because you seem more and more argumentative these days. Maybe that's a sign of you getting better.

May 31, 2015

Dear Daddy,

Well, it looks like it's time for me to go back to my house and back to work. You seem to be okay taking your medication. I know you have some friends and family who will be my eyes for me when possible.

We rode up to Northern Virginia with Anita in the car with us. Fortunately, she didn't say too much.

When it was time to drop me off and let you head back to Hampton with Anita, it was hard. It felt like I was leaving my child. I could see it in your eyes too, but you had to do this to show that you can handle this. I have to believe that I have put all the right things in place for you to be okay.

We took a selfie before you left.

As I stayed home for the first time in a long time, I had to reflect on our time together. It was hard, but I am so honored that I got to be there with you. I thought about some who weren't so lucky. We had an okay relationship before all of this, but it got stronger as you were shown that you could trust me. It was me and you. And we got through this ordeal together.

I love you, Dad.

About the Author

Shaunté Newby, also known as Shaunté Says, is a certified life coach, career strategist, and voice actor.

Recognizing that her life experiences and observations are not only for her and can truly help others, she launched an organization called I'm Built for This that reminds her clients that they are built for whatever their "this" is.

Often commended for her approach to taking care of her father, she also helps those who unexpectedly land one of the most memorable and important roles in their lives, the caregiver.